ENDORSEMENT

"We are great believers in real estate investments, and our mission is to help real estate investors create income to live life on their terms. A high level of Financial Literacy is one of the key ingredients that our real estate investors need to be successful—to understand how to make money work for them. This is why we love how Ingrid's book shares her journey to become financially literate as a result of her desire to become a successful Real Estate Investor, and the impact that a higher level of Financial Intelligence had on her success in Real Estate Investing. Another thing that stood out for us is the real-life examples relating to personal finance that she shares, which can be easily understood and applied to everyone's lives to help them avoid bad debt and manage their money effectively to improve their financial situation."

—**Tom and Nick Karadza,** The Real Estate Investment Experts, Founders of ROCK STAR Real Estate Inc, International Bestselling Authors of *Income for Life—for Canadians*

"I love Ingrid's Book! I've been a professional speaker, writer, and corporate trainer for over 25 years. As a business owner, I know with certainty that a high level of Financial Intelligence is required to run a successful business, and a successful life. I believe financial education should be mandatory for every high school student. This is why I really love that, in her book, Ingrid shares her observations and experiences as an educator who initially had limited financial education, as well as the impact that financial education had on her personal success and achievements after she became more financially savvy.

I also love that she uses simple examples from her lived experiences that every reader can relate to easily, and explains how everyone can play their part to improve their Financial Intelligence and promote Financial Literacy among the masses."

—**James MacNeil,** The REAL Love Guru, International Bestselling Author and Founder of Pure Spiritual Intelligence and Verbal Aikido, CEO of EQ Communications Inc.

"Being a wholistic health and wellness authority, I know that low academic performance, poor money management and a weak financial foundation can lead to anxiety and stress for many individuals and families. Extended periods of stress relating to poor grades and financial instability can take their toll and have a negative effect on people's physical, mental and emotional health. I love how Ingrid explains the importance of getting good grades, but also why good grades aren't enough to build a strong financial foundation to achieve great success and improve your overall well-being. I also like that she explains why Financial Literacy is paramount, and why school should play a significant role in ensuring that students leave high school financially educated, to empower them to become more financially successful and improve their quality of life."

—**Dr. Stacey Cooper,** Founder of Lifestyle Balance Solutions and Creator of the Balanced Living Summit, and 90 Day New You. International Bestselling Author of *What's Self Love Got to Do With It?* and *Heal Your Health Naturally*

GOOD GRADES ROCK!! BUT A⁺ ≠ $UCCE$$

Why School Should Teach You Financial Literacy

INGRID B. CLAYTON

Good Grades Rock!! But A⁺ ≠ $UCCE$$
Why School Should Teach You Financial Literacy

www.goodgradesrock.com

Copyright © 2020 Ingrid B. Clayton

ISBN: 978-1-77277-379-8

All rights reserved. No portion of this book may be reproduced mechanically, electronically, or by any other means, including photocopying, without permission of the publisher or author except in the case of brief quotations embodied in critical articles and reviews. It is illegal to copy this book, post it to a website, or distribute it by any other means without permission from the author or publisher.

Limits of Liability and Disclaimer of Warranty

The author and publisher shall not be liable for your misuse of the enclosed material. This book is strictly for informational and educational purposes only. The author and publisher have made every effort to ensure that the information contained in this book to be correct at the time of publication; however, neither the author nor the publisher assumes any responsibility for the outcome of any of the information in this book.

Warning – Disclaimer

The purpose of this book is to educate and entertain. The author and/or publisher do not guarantee that anyone following these techniques, suggestions, tips, ideas, or strategies will become successful. The author and/or publisher shall have neither liability nor responsibility to anyone with respect to any loss or damage caused, or alleged to be caused, directly or indirectly by the information contained in this book.

Financial Disclaimer

This book is written for Canada and the United States. Although there are similarities in the financial and economic systems in both countries, there are some differences regarding products and services. But the key financial concepts about money and how it works are the same. The purpose of this book is to provide information and give a general understanding about financial concepts. It's not intended to give advice on investment, insurance, tax, accounting or any financial products or services. The views and opinions expressed in this book are those of the author, and should not be used as a substitute for professional financial advice.

By reading this book you acknowledge your understanding and acceptance of the disclaimer.

Publisher
10-10-10 Publishing
Markham, ON Canada

Printed in Canada and the United States of America

DEDICATION

This book is dedicated to you and your brothers and sisters, and to all the young people, parents, teachers, and other stakeholders who will carry the baton to spread the importance of financial education and why it should be included in every school curriculum.

I thank you for taking the time to start changing the world by taking the first step. I hope you will use some of the great ideas and examples that I share here to increase your financial intelligence and the financial intelligence of all the lives that you can impact.

"The two most important days in your life are the day you are born and the day you find out why."

—Mark Twain

CONTENTS

ACKNOWLEDGEMENTS XIII
FOREWORD XIX

1. GOOD GRADES MATTER 1
   The Grade Effect 3
   Can You Measure Learning? 6
   Is School About Learning or Getting Good Grades? 10
   The Standardized Testing Effect 14
   The Up and Downside of Good Grades 17
   Is Failing Bad? What Grade Says You're Smart? 21

2. THE HIGH SCHOOL MATH CURRICULUM 25
   How People View the Math Curriculum 27
   What Math Is Useful to Everyone? 29
   The Math Curriculum and the Real World 31
   Is the Math Curriculum Changing to Match the Real world? 33
   Which Professions Need Intense Math? 34
   Why Is Math a Prerequisite? 37

3. MY EXPERIENCE AS A MATH TEACHER 39
   Why Students Are Disengaged 41
      What is causing this trend? 42
   Why Many Students Struggle with Math 44
      Back to My Essential Math Class 47
   The Greatest Barriers for Math Learners 48

    The Vocabulary 48
    The Syntax 49
    The Formulas 49
    The Problem-Solving Process 50
    Learning Gaps 50
    Irrelevant Curriculum 51
  Challenges in the Math Classroom 51
    Large Class Size 52
    Teacher Training 52
    Students' Disengagement 53
  How Can the Math Curriculum Be More Relevant? 54
  Should High School Math Be Optional? 57

4. **FINANCIAL LITERACY IS MISSING** 61
  The School Curriculum Needs Overhauling 63
  Why Financial Literacy Should Be Included 66
  A Short Conversation with a Tenant Applicant 69
  Students Have More Interest in Money 71
  Why Some Topics Engage Students More 73
  Why More Focus on Financial Applications
  Will Interest Students 76
  Why Math Should Emphasize More Real-Life
  Application Concepts 77
    What's the lesson here? 79

5. **FINANCIAL LITERACY MATTERS** 81
  Managing Household Expenses 83
  Buying a Home 85
  Saving for Emergency Expenses 88
  Saving for Your Children's Education 90

  Can this be avoided? 92
  Student Loan Interest Rate 94
 Investing in Yourself 96
  What is "Bank on Yourself"? 97
  Another Bank on Yourself Example 98
 Investing for Your Retirement 99
  What is a self-directed RRSP? 101

6. TEACHING YOUNG PEOPLE FINANCIAL LITERACY 103
 Creating a Budget 105
 Managing Your Credit Cards 107
 Building and Protecting Your Credit 110
 Lines of Credit Vs Credit Cards 114
 Using Insurance to Increase Wealth 117
  Whole Life Insurance 118
  Universal Life Insurance 119
 Investing in Your Future 121
  Investing in Education/Coaching/Mentoring 122
  Investing in a Business 122
  Investing in Real Estate 123
  Investing in a Retirement Savings Plan 123

7. I REALIZED I NEEDED FINANCIAL EDUCATION 127
 I Thought I Knew Enough 129
 A Wake-Up Call 131
 The Effect of Change 135
 Why A⁺ in Math ≠ Financial Literacy 138
 Where You Should Learn Financial Literacy 140
 The Mistakes I Could Have Avoided 144

8. **MY JOURNEY TO BECOME FINANCIALLY INTELLIGENT** 149
   - I Learned More Outside the Classroom 151
   - The Difference Between a Job and Making Money 153
   - Assets Vs Liability 155
   - Good Debt vs Bad Debt 156
   - How I Made Money from Credit Cards 161
   - Using Other People's Money to Build Wealth 163

9. **WHAT I ACCOMPLISHED AFTER BECOMING FINANCIALLY LITERATE** 167
   - Increasing My Assets and Limiting My Liabilities 169
   - The Power of Negotiation 171
   - The Ability to Help Others 173
   - Peace of Mind 176
   - Living Life on My Terms 179
   - Leaving a Legacy 181

10. **THE DEBT CRISIS CONSUMERS FACE** 185
    - What Is Government Doing? 187
    - Your Children Will Carry the Burden 190
        - *Debt Consolidation* 191
        - *Pay More Frequently* 192
        - *Make Lump Sum Payments* 192
        - *Pay Off Debts With Shorter Time First* 193
    - Tracking Your Expenses Helps 193
    - Buying Smart Helps 196
        - *Shopping for Food Items* 196
        - *What about other purchases?* 197
    - Avoid Consumer Debt 198
        - *Buy What Is Needed* 198

  Emergency Funds 198
  Be Smart With Credit Cards 199
  Cash Advances and Balance Transfers 200
  Limit Your Exposure 200
  Be Smart With Lines of Credit 201
  Line of Credit Example 201
  Credit Card Example 202
 Start Your Financial Literacy Journey 203

11. IT'S TIME FOR CHANGE 207
 Who Is Giving You Financial Advice? 209
 Focus on What's Applicable 211
 Teach Children About Money and Entrepreneurship 213
 Spread the Importance of Financial Education 216
 Dare to Leave a Legacy 218
  Life Insurance 219
  Education Savings Plan 220
  Retirement Savings Plan 221
  Business Investments 221
  Having a Will 222
  Financial Education 222
 Financial Literacy Should Be Mandatory in Schools 223
 Attend Free Financial Education Workshops 227

RECOMMENDED READING LIST 229
ABOUT INGRID B. CLAYTON 233
ABOUT THIS BOOK 235

ACKNOWLEDGEMENTS

To my husband, **Richard Clayton,** who is my rock and number one cheerleader. He has been by my side for more than 24 years, and without him, none of this would be possible. He kept encouraging and cheering me on even when I felt like giving up. When I felt tired and overwhelmed and started to wonder if anyone will even listen, he remained positive and provided many reasons why writing this book is definitely a great idea. He also shared why it will help others to change their mindset about money to improve their finances and thus increase their standard of living. Thank you for being patient, feeding me when I get engrossed and forget to eat, and for loving me unconditionally.

To my two wonderful sons, **Kyle** and **Cody**, who also cheered me on, and thought it was cool that I wanted to write about something that was very important and could impact people's lives. Thank you for being patient and for not holding it against me when I had no time to hang out with you because I was too immersed in my research and writing. And a special thank you to Kyle, who helped me to structure some sentences that just didn't capture the essence of what I wanted to say.

To my mother, **Viviene Scott**, who encouraged me, believed in me, supported me, and made me believe I can do anything that I put my mind to. The question, *How much more to go now*? kept me going so that I would have something different to answer each time. Thank you for the daily prayers that you keep sending up to heaven for me, especially when you're not physically present to help in my times of need. I love you Mumzel!

To my mother-in-law and second mother, **Brenda Clayton**, who loves me as her own daughter—perhaps even more—and keeps our home functioning, preparing meals, talking with the boys, and keeping the home in tip-top shape when I'm too busy to play the homemaker role. To my father-in-law, **Winston Clayton**, who has been more than a dad to me. I've gained many insights and wisdom from him, from our little laughs and talks. Thank you for the daily encouraging and motivational words you send that remind me, especially at a low point in my life, that I can write this book. You are both wonderful parents to me, and I love you both dearly.

To my sister-in-law, **Ramona Clayton,** who takes care of my boys when Richard and I go on vacations, or takes care of our home, plants, and flowers when Richard and I take off with the boys. Thank you for babysitting and house sitting so that we can have peace of mind whenever we're away.

To my brother, **Horace Beckford,** who keeps my company every morning as I drive to school, and gives me that boost of energy each morning by getting me to laugh for most of my journey, even when I'm exhausted from staying up too late writing. Thank you for the gift of love and friendship.

To my aunt and uncle, **Lady Patricia Allen** and **Sir Patrick Allen**, the First Lady and Governor General of Jamaica, who gave me the gift of love and taught me how to forgive and let go. Thank you for loving me and enabling me to see that no dream is too big to pursue.

To **Winston Senior** and **Dennis Grant** for your special friendship that means the world to me. Thank you for the great talks and laughs, and for always cheering me on. Your unconditional love and continuous support are dear to my heart.

Acknowledgements

To all my friends and family members—**Amoy McPherson, O'Neil McPherson, Cavel Young, Winston Senior, Claudia Smith, Carleen Anderson, Sherwin Aarons, Jeffery Melbourne, Dr. Kenneth Montague, Dr. Douglas Jefferson**—in various professions, who allowed me to interview them to determine the percentage of high school and university math they use in their current profession.

To my professor, **Randee Lawrence**, who made me believe I was selling myself short in thinking I couldn't write a book. The words, *"I'm hoping to read that book one day,"* kept playing over and over in my head until I eventually caved and started to write. Thank you for planting that seed in my mind.

To my former principal, **Valerie Nelson**, who made me believe that people will listen to me even if I'm saying what they don't want to hear. You helped me to understand that it's not just about what I say but how I say it, and the passion that echoes through my voice and my choice of words. Thank you for encouraging me to be a leader.

To my principal, **Denise De Paola**, who helped me to build my capacity and grow as a leader. Thank you for taking a chance on me and for providing me with the knowledge and the guidance to be bold and fearless, and for sharing my vision to financially educate our students.

To all my co-workers, especially my co-ACL, **Carmen Ku**, who helped me with resources, writing evaluations, marking, and other school-related activities. Thank you for all your help and encouragement and for supporting the importance of financial literacy, and for sharing the belief that financial education should be taught in school.

To **Tom Karadza** and **Nick Karadza** (Income for Life) for your teachings, inspiration, and your tenacity to keep sharing with and helping real estate investors to score big. I've learned so much about real estate investing and personal development from you both. Thank you for building a community of like-minded people that I can be a part of.

To my real estate coach, **John Paul Hunt**, who was a great support and source of encouragement when I started my real estate investing journey. Your knowledge, wisdom, guidance, and patience helped me to find the ideal properties to grow my real estate portfolio and build my confidence as an investor. Thank you for being there at the beginning of my journey and for continuing to be a great help today.

To my friend, **Dr. Stacey** (Heal Your Health), who was a great source of encouragement. Her energy, motivation, and words of encouragement made me believe that I could complete this book. Thank you for those great Facebook posts that help me to keep the momentum going.

To my friend, **James MacNeil (Pure Spiritual Intelligence)**, who was a great source of encouragement. He made me believe that I am perfect in my personhood, and that my dream life is already made and waiting for me. He enabled me to see that I am destined for great things, and that the best is yet to come. Thank you for believing that everyone can dream big and achieve their dream life.

To **Chinmai Swamy, Liz Ventrella,** and **Wasqas Ahmed,** whose suggestions, help, and guidance made this physical book a reality.

To **Lisa Browning,** my editor and formatter.

To my publisher, **Raymond Aaron**, who is a great teacher and advisor, and who created a clear road map for me to follow so that I could complete my book. You enabled me to break down this mammoth task of writing this

Acknowledgements

book, into manageable bite-size pieces that definitely avoid writer's block, like you said. Without you, this book would still be a dream waiting to come to fruition. Because of you, I am now an award winner of two books, and my mission has begun. Thank you for the great teachings and guidance.

FOREWORD

It has always been rather mind-boggling to me that a subject as important as financial education is not taught in school. This is why I am really moved by Ingrid's enthusiasm and mission to expose you to financial education. Ingrid has been a high school teacher for her entire working life of twenty-three years. She's very enthusiastic about teaching and preparing you for future success. Ingrid recognized from early adulthood that, despite being an A+ math student, she needed financial education to achieve her goals for financial independence, and success for herself and her loved ones. This knowledge caused her to embark on a financial education journey to increase her financial IQ and put her financial intelligence to the test.

In Ingrid's book, *Good Grades Rock But A+ ≠ $ucce$$*, you will gain insight as to why having excellent grades doesn't necessarily lead to financial success. Ingrid shares how financial education, and changing your mindset about money and how you manage it effectively, can help you to build a strong financial foundation. She uses simple examples and stories from her lived experience to show you how to become financially successful.

Ingrid also shares that you can do your part in helping to relieve the high consumer debt looming in your country, by becoming financially educated, and teaching your children about money. Get ready to read this amazing book that will teach you how to put your own finances in order, so that you can build a strong financial foundation on which to build your dream life. The sooner you begin, the better off you'll be in the future!

—Raymond Aaron
New York Times Bestselling Author

1
Good Grades Matter

"School, I never truly got the knack of. I could never focus on things I didn't want to learn. Math is just the worst. To this day, I can't concentrate on it. People always say, 'You should have tried harder.' But actually, I cheated a lot because I could not sit and do homework."

—Leonardo DiCaprio

The Grade Effect

In real life, the world is your classroom. You learn from your experiences and observations, you learn from each other, you learn from trial and error, taking chances and risks, and you learn from your own and others' mistakes. Just think about the progression of the first few years of your life. You learned to creep, walk, climb, run, talk, count, write, read, and many more things without having to write a test or an exam. You were never given a grade to tell you how well you were doing at these things. And when you failed at any of them, you didn't feel like it was a bad thing. You would pick yourself up and keep going, and mom and dad would keep cheering you on. Moreover, you were also willing to try everything you could conceive of; you thought you were the smartest kid, you had no fear, and the world was your playing ground for you to try whatever came to your mind.

A few years later, something changed; school happened. Suddenly, you became fearful to explore, you no longer wanted to take risks, you stopped thinking you're the smartest kid, and failure became your worst enemy. Your skills and ability started to be judged by the grade you received on a task you were expected to complete within a specified time, and in a controlled environment. Do you think you took the same amount of time to learn how to walk, talk, and count as everyone else? Do you think you walk, talk, and count better than those who took longer to accomplish these feats? I believe, except for those with an impairment, everyone walks, talks, and counts just fine, despite the time taken to accomplish them. But in school, you're given time constraints to demonstrate your learning, and you're given a grade whether you complete your task or not. But why? Would a company deliver unfinished products to its clients? What feedback would be expected from the client?

And what if you were the student who felt like your world was shattered when you received an unexpectedly low grade on a test? If your grades were below what your parents expected, were you excited taking it home to show them, or did you always feel anxious because you didn't want to see the disappointment on their faces? And if your teacher required a parent's signature, when your mark was unsatisfactory, how many times did your teacher have to ask you to return the signed test before you eventually got it signed? Perhaps there were even times you asked an older sibling or a friend to sign your test, because you didn't want to show it to your parents. You did this because you wanted to avoid seeing the disappointment on their faces.

My teachers didn't require a signature on my tests, but there was an unspoken expectation that my parents should see all my marked evaluations so they could keep abreast with my progress. In fact, even if I never had that understanding, my mom was actively involved in my school life, so if I inadvertently forgot to show her, before long, she would have asked when the next test would be, or when the last test I wrote would be returned. My mom had never stipulated what mark was an acceptable performance for her, but there was an unexpressed tone that anything less than an A meant I needed to do better.

As a result, if I didn't get an A, I felt disappointed and I became anxious. And whenever I scored less than an A, I didn't feel that I was as smart as when I got A's. There were times I even second guessed myself, thinking that maybe I wasn't as smart as I thought. It was even more devastating when friends, who regularly looked to me for help, occasionally outperformed me. Whenever that happened, I would complain about how unfair life was, because a friend or two that I had helped, had received a higher grade than I did. I felt perplexed because, deep down, I knew I'd grasped the concepts more quickly, and had deeper learning since I could effectively explain what I learned to others. There were even times I vowed not to help anyone again, although that didn't pan out. As a student, I loved helping others to understand concepts they had difficulty with, and perhaps that is why I became a teacher.

What I learned later in my academic career was that external factors were mitigating against my performance on evaluations. Tests made me very anxious, and I was somewhat a perfectionist, so I would spend too much time obsessing about writing neatly and checking over each question before moving on to the next. For this reason, there were very few times I actually completed my tests. At the end of the day, however, none of those debilitating factors mattered. The grade I received on a test, told the world how smart I was. And nothing a doctor or I could say, would have changed that fact. However, I knew deep down that my grades weren't a true reflection of my learning, and some of my teachers would share that as well. But because so much emphasis was placed on grades and my rank in the class, actual learning sometimes seemed secondary. To make matters worse, my class ranking was limited to my performance on evaluations. Luckily for me, I would perform very well on the portions of the tests I completed, so I was always ranked at the top, and I was viewed as a high performing student.

But what about you, who may have poor test-taking skills, and who didn't necessarily perform as well on the questions you completed? What about you, who may suffer from anxieties that are triggered by having to write a test? Do you ever experience a favourable test day? Were test days stress-free or over-stressed days? How can the grade you receive on over-stressed days demonstrate your true learning? One parent shared at a parent night meet that her son had math test anxiety. No other subject except math triggered his anxiety and gave him nightmares on the nights leading up to his test. And for this reason, he always performs poorly on tests, despite the strong ability he displays during class.

Unfortunately, we live in a culture where grades are used to dictate your ability or how smart you are. And society often uses it to judge how successful you will become in the future. While I agree that getting good grades is great, since they can win you awards and scholarships, help you to get into competitive programs, make you the preferred candidate for a job position, and so on, I don't believe that a grade necessarily demonstrates your true academic ability. I also don't think that it reflects your true level of learning, or that it measures how successful you will become later in life. As Deese and Deese said in their book, *How to Study and Other Skills for Success in College*, grades are only one imperfect reflection of how much you have learned in your various courses. People can have deep learning and acquire a good education without receiving high grades; while on the other hand, there are students who make straight A's, who concentrate so much on getting them that they miss their education. They cannot think outside the box because they aim to keep perfecting the box. Perhaps this is why Robert Kiyosaki said that A-students usually work for C-students. C-students are more about how they can get around or stay outside the box, and they love to employ the A-students to perfect things in their business boxes.

Can You Measure Learning?

Does your grade represent how much you have learned? Do a mental reflection, and determine if you think your grades reflect your real learning. On multiple occasions, when I was a student, I felt that my mark didn't accurately represent my actual learning. And not only mine, because there were times when some of my classmates received lower grades than others, but I believed the lower performing ones demonstrated more mastery of subject content than their counterparts who received higher marks. In fact, I've encountered many students like these throughout my teaching career. Perhaps you are one of them. These are the students who usually complain that I'm always on their case to improve their test-taking skills to perform better on evaluations.

Why do I always pressure them to perform better? Because I believe, if they live in a society where grades are often used to dictate mastery of subject content, and if students have the ability to obtain nineties, they shouldn't be settling for eighties. And since grades often determine if you're eligible to pursue a particular career program at college or university, getting lower grades may not put them in the cream of the crop. So, I bought into the idea that you shouldn't be settling for mediocre grades when you can demonstrate to the world that you definitely have what it takes. This, I believe, provides you with better options to pick, choose, and refuse whatever you want to pursue in your life.

But to some extent, I was that student. I had poor test-taking skills, I had test anxiety issues, and I rarely completed my tests. For these reasons, my marks were usually affected due to incomplete work, not a lack of knowledge. My older brother, on the other hand, was very different. My mom would always brag about his A⁺ report cards, and although I was always a high performing student, I just accepted that he was the genius of the family. However, when I had the opportunity to spend some time with him (he was living with his dad then), I would notice how dedicated he was to getting A⁺ grades at all costs. He would spend hours studying, and he would complete every practice question, whether assigned or not. And then I thought to myself that maybe he wasn't a pure genius after all; he was outperforming me because he spent 110% of his time studying.

To test my theory, I decided to put more effort into my work, and I started spending more time practicing and studying. Not surprisingly, I began to see improvement in my marks. However, the downside was that I couldn't sustain that stance because that is not naturally who I am, and it had its effect. I love my downtime, so over time I would slack off again, thinking that my natural performance was acceptable after all, so why the extra stress? But it was great knowing that despite the debilitating factors, I could get better grades if I pushed myself even harder. But pushing myself more impacted my well being. I would stay up later, trying to practice more questions, thus reducing my sleep time, which made me very cranky in the mornings. And I would spend little or no time playing board games—which I enjoyed doing—with friends and family members.

Despite my personal preference, however, I do want my students to recognize that they are capable of getting better grades when they apply more effort. Had I not had the opportunity to observe my brother's ways, I wouldn't have believed that I was capable of performing better on assessments despite my anxieties. Hence, I want my students to know that a lower or failing grade doesn't define them. And they don't have to resort to cheating or copying from others to receive a more acceptable mark. When they are aware, and believe that they can do better, they won't get demotivated easily, and their self-esteem won't get crushed whenever they see a low mark. I strive to help them to understand that failing is not bad. And while they may interpret failure as they didn't learn something as well as they thought they did, ultimately, it means they just need to focus on the feedback and try again.

And yes, they may need more time to grasp the concepts, and another opportunity to demonstrate their learning, but it doesn't mean they're not smart, or that they're stupid and cannot learn, as some of them have said. The drawback, however, is that school gives students a limited time to complete the curriculum, so they are herded from class to class, at the ring of a bell, with not enough time to reflect, practice, and process what they learned in one class before having to sit in another one. Studies have shown that if you don't practice what you learn soon after, it will not stick. So the million-dollar question is: Did students not learn enough, or was the problem that they didn't have enough time to process what they learned to store it away in memory?

For instance, English Language was always my worst course in school. My English Language teacher used to say that I couldn't write a good essay or story if my life depended on it. That was rather strange because my English Literature marks were always very good. But I'd heard it often enough, and my English Language grades were always low, so I just accepted that as fact. And it didn't really bother me either; as long as I got 60%—the amount needed to pass in my time—I was satisfied. The first time I did my external English exam, I failed. I wasn't surprised, because a considerable chunk of the mark came from writing an essay and a story on the exam, and I'd conceded that I wasn't good at it.

However, I knew I needed to pass the external exam before my final year, and I was determined to pass it on the second try. I had already tested the theory that my grade doesn't necessarily demonstrate my true ability, so I knew what I had to do. Hence, I decided to quit settling for mediocre marks in this course. So, I ramped up my efforts, and put in more quality time. When I got the results, I wasn't surprised that I had passed. I knew I hadn't learned anything new in the course, but I spent more time processing and applying what I'd learned prior, and that made all the difference. Although I didn't like the subject, I got a better grade because I decided to be more positive, put in more effort, and apply myself better. This strategy can work for you too; a mark doesn't dictate your ability—more effort and perseverance can make a huge difference.

Is School About Learning or Getting Good Grades?

When I was writing this page, I tried to reflect back to my schooling years to determine if I've always felt like the main goal in school was to learn or to get good grades. Was there a time when I was more focused on learning instead of on the marks I could show my parents? My memory could be playing tricks on me, but somehow I feel like my first four years of elementary school were more focused on learning, but things changed drastically after that. While grades were definitely crucial for a report card at the end of each year, during the course of the year, I believe the focus was more on preparing me to be a better reader, be better at arithmetic, to improve my grammar, to learn about geography and social studies, and to improve my penmanship. Grades became a primary goal in the latter part of my elementary school years, when my teacher started preparing me to write a standardized test that would determine which high school I would attend. Since I was determined to go to the top high school in my town, I knew I had to get good grades; hence, there was a shift in my paradigm.

Thereafter, my focus continued to be on grades because, while I was easily one of the top students in my elementary school, high school was a different ball game. My first high school class had multiple top students from various elementary schools, so my efforts had to be significantly improved to remain in the top 10. In fact, in high school, we got two report cards instead of one. And I can remember the first question my mom asked after I received my first high school report card: "How much did you rank in your class?" Without even looking at my grades, I could see the slight disappointment on her face when she discovered I was no longer in the top three. I had to explain to her that it wasn't like elementary school anymore; my class had top students from different schools, but my grades were still good. Once she took the time to look at my grades, I saw that her face softened.

I don't know if the lesson I took from that episode was good or bad, but at that moment, I started to believe that my mom cared more about my grades than on my ranking in the class. So, the rest of my high school career was focused on learning and doing well, to hit the grades I believed she was satisfied with. However, throughout the years, I still disliked writing tests and exams, especially because I thought they brought on unnecessary stress and anxiety. And for this reason, over time, a lot of my focus shifted to: What will be on the test or exam? What can I do to master this test-taking and exam-writing thing better? The question of whether I had learned this concept thoroughly, became infrequent. And I became more obsessed with completing questions on previous tests and exams than with learning.

Of course, I never mastered the art of test-taking or writing exams to this day, so in some sense those efforts were futile; but that caused me to question why grades are often determined from standardized tests that are written in a very controlled environment with time constraints. While you're allowed to do your homework at your own pace, with your textbooks, your notes, and being a phone call away from friends or relatives to help you, as well as now having the internet at your fingertips, you're expected to complete your evaluations in a specified time. Sometimes you're also required to write them in an unfamiliar room. Would you feel more comfortable writing your exam in *your* home, or your neighbour's home?

Who came up with this testing and grading strategy? Why do you need to demonstrate your learning within a specified time? On your math tests, for instance, you may read the instructions and the questions at a slower rate than your friends do. You may even write much slower than them. Your thought process of selecting the necessary tools/strategies to solve a problem may even be slower than theirs, so why do you all get the same time to complete your tests? You would think it's a marathon to see who can get to the finish line the fastest. Except your grade is not based on how fast you arrive, but on the running strategies, and the techniques you utilized along the way.

And perhaps some may argue that if you do things more slowly, then you might need an Individualised Learning Plan (IEP). So your teacher should have referred you for an assessment, so others can decide what they think you need or don't need. You cannot speak for yourself and, sometimes, if all your teachers aren't seeing the same trend in their classes, then you're not entitled to extra time. I was an excellent math student, and yet I know I could have gotten higher grades in math had I been given time to complete every question. There were times when I felt that even an extra five minutes would have made a whole lot of difference in my mark. What about you—did you ever feel like something clicked when your teacher announced that the bell would be going in five minutes? Did something click within the last two minutes, but it felt pointless even to begin the question because you knew that two minutes were not sufficient to finish it?

So, my next two questions are: Is writing evaluations really a strategy to demonstrate your authentic learning and ability, or is it a technique utilized to help determine a grade for your report cards, and whether you're eligible to pursue study in a particular program? Is school focused more on learning`` or more focused on testing and grading? There are times when I feel like my students spend more time focused on writing evaluations and worrying about marks, than they do on learning. And a lot of the evaluations students get are variants of standardized testing, even though they are mostly administered in their classroom. You may be asking: Why do you let your students write standardized assessments, if you're not in favour of them? My response to that is: For a subject like math, for instance, evaluating students is a part of my job responsibility, and I'm expected to test them under similar conditions, so that I can report a mark on their report card. In fact, within school boards, schools are often ranked according to how their students perform on standardized assessments.

Although a lot of focus is placed on grade, grading and learning are definitely not the same thing. There's way more to learning than a grade can capture. The flawed method of grading has been around since the Industrial Age, and nothing seems to be changing much. If your grade should represent how much you know and have learned, then you should be tested under conditions that make you feel relaxed and comfortable, so that you can optimize your performance. And the same time constraint should not be imposed on everyone, especially when the time taken to complete homework, classwork, and assignments are not the same for each student. While I understand that reporting students' performance is important, and that there is a limited time for classroom assessments and evaluations, the current high school system, in many countries, is not designed to capture students' ultimate academic success. With a level playing field, students who score C's could have been just as successful as those who score A's. Perhaps a new method for testing students is needed, and it's not only about giving students extra time; a lot should be considered as to how students perceive writing evaluations, and the impact it has on them and their performance.

The Standardized Testing Effect

Why does the education system, in many countries, encourage standardized assessments for students? Why can't you be allowed to write the test at your own pace, to demonstrate your ultimate learning? Moreover, the assessment itself can be a barrier for you and others. For example, you may not like multiple-choice questions, while others may not like long response questions. Reports state that when Frederick J. Kelly invented standardized testing, in the early twentieth century, the goal wasn't so much to measure learning but more to streamline schooling to avoid overpopulation. One of the reports also states that when he realized that the test was too crude and needed to be abandoned, he argued for a change in the way students' learning is assessed. As his views weren't popular among key stakeholders, he was asked to step down as president of the faculty at the college he was working at the time. Today, many schools are still using some variation of the outdated standardized test that Kelly designed more than a century ago. The world has been changing from the Industrial Age to the Technological Age, for more than half a century, but it seems the education system is still very much in the Industrial Age.

And don't get me wrong; I too am guilty of employing that same form of standardized testing to my students, but as the saying goes, *when you're in Rome, you do as the Romans do*. But it doesn't mean I haven't challenged the status quo along the way. Let me share one example of how I've tried to change my practice but was overridden by the masses. One year, I had a student who was transferred from academic math to my enriched math class. Before long, I noticed that he worked slower than my original enriched students, but he was obviously a strong student. On occasions, before answering, he would say, "Hold on Ms.," even though multiple hands were already up and wagging, eager to provide the answer. While this meant that he needed more time to arrive at his answer, more than 95% of the time, his response was correct.

When he wrote his first test, he asked for an extra five minutes to complete a question, and he got 4 out of the 5 marks for the problem. On his second test, he asked for some extra time again. Some of the other students were looking on, and their facial expressions indicated they were thinking it wasn't fair that he was allowed extra time. Thereafter, I spoke to his vice principal about him needing additional time, and I was told that I had to follow protocol and refer him to the team that assesses students' needs. After the meeting, the report said that the student is not entitled to extra time because his other teachers saw no need for it. In a further discussion, one comment was made that perhaps the enriched class was not the right fit for the student, because he shouldn't get special treatment. I felt defeated…it wasn't that the student was asking for a whole lot of extra time. And not needing additional time in other subject areas, doesn't translate to not needing extra time to complete his math evaluations.

A few weeks later, I received an email saying that the student should be excused from class whenever symptoms of a medical condition surfaced, even when he was writing a test. I got excited, thinking that it was great news, because his situation could very well be impacting his test writing speed in math. Hence, I could afford him the extra time without getting a backlash from his classmates. Soon after, I was told that despite the student's situation, he wasn't entitled to time beyond how long he left the room. His vice principal was very understanding, however, and recommended I use my own discretion. Suffice to say, I always felt relieved whenever the student needed to leave during the test, because I never took note of the time, and I knew the other students weren't taking notes either. So, upon returning, I would allow him to complete his test.

A later conversation with the student's mother confirmed that math caused him to be anxious because he wanted to do very well in the enriched class, and that was one of the triggers for his symptoms. I encouraged his mom to register him in the *After School Numeracy Program*, so that he could improve his speed by having additional opportunities to practice. Suffice to say, that student completed the course with a much higher mark than some of his classmates who were originally enriched students. His time wasn't standardized, and that afforded him the opportunity to work at a more comfortable pace and demonstrate his true potential.

It is evident that the current method that is pervasively used in our education system, to administer evaluations, needs some work. It should not be a one-size-fits-all practice, because the rate at which students complete tasks varies. And just because they may require a bit more time to demonstrate their learning, doesn't necessarily mean that they have a learning disability or need an IEP. It may take you five minutes to read this page, while it may take another reader ten minutes. But does that necessarily mean that you're a better reader and learner than the other person? What if you can both recount the same content on the page after reading? That would mean that you're just faster, but you both achieve the same outcome. And it's also possible that the slower reader may recount more than you do, or the other way around, but I believe you get my point.

My high school teachers in Jamaica had no knowledge about what was on my final year exams, and teachers from different countries marked the exams. Imagine all your final high school exams being treated like a traditional standardized test. Depending on where you attended high school, you may be familiar with this evaluation system. There was no concept of a medical note, so if you were sick and couldn't write your exam, you weren't allowed to re-write a day or so later. And if you were having a horrible day on the day of an exam, and did poorly on just that exam, that low mark could set back your university career for a whole year. There was no option to upgrade in summer school or night school, like we have in Canada. If you failed a course, you would have to wait until the following year to rewrite that exam, because each exam was administered once per year, on the same day, across the country. While this system may not exist in Canada or America, other countries in the world still employ it. I've had international students who pay top dollars to study in Canada, because they want better opportunities than what the traditional standardized testing technique affords them in their own countries. But, although the assessment system may be less rigid in some countries, there is still need for improvement across the board.

The Up and Downside of Good Grades

A traditional view that is shared by the masses is that academic success is tantamount to lifelong success. Go to school and get good grades so that you can get a good job and take care of yourself and your family later in life, I was told. I heard it so often that when I began reading about successful people like Walt Disney, Steve Jobs, Thomas Edison, and Bill Gates, who were school dropouts, I wondered how that could be possible when their parents weren't wealthy. Later on, when I read more books, like *The 7 Habits of Highly Effective People,* by Stephen Covey, *Think and Grow Rich*, by Napoleon Hill, and the *Rich Dad Poor Dad* series by Robert Kiyosaki, I began to understand more and more why success is not about getting A+. There's way more to success than a grade. It also helped me to understand why many C-students become entrepreneurs, while A-students focus more on getting a prestigious position at a Fortune 500 company. C-students are more business oriented; they focus more on running their own business and owning their own companies. That is not to say that A-students are not successful and are not entrepreneurs. But frequently, they are the sum total of the experts in large corporations, who have the prestigious titles, instead of being the owners of the businesses.

Three main characteristics that all successful people have, are risk-taking, perseverance, and the determination to keep learning. They don't quit at the first sign of failure, and they don't waste time trying to avoid failures. They keep persevering while learning from their mistakes, and they aspire to acquire the necessary skills to achieve their goals. Is it possible that everyone can achieve great success in academics and the real world if they make these characteristics become a part of their lives? Sometimes you underestimate your true potential, and limit yourself so that you can blend in with the masses. You don't want to be viewed as different, so you prefer to be average. *"I don't want to spend too much time studying Ms., because my friends will think I'm a nerd."* That was what one of my students told me when I asked if he had practiced the word problems for a math test. My response to him was: *"If you're doing what everybody else is doing, you will end up where everyone else is."*

Can you remember a time in your life when you received a mark much higher than what you were expecting, a mark that may have ranked you higher than a friend who you thought was smarter than you? What went through your mind then? Did you think you were smarter than you thought? Did you think your teacher may have made a mistake with tabulating the marks? What did it do for your self-esteem? Did it motivate you to work harder to obtain that mark again? My guess is that you thought it was just a fluke, or an anomaly that may never occur again. I suspect you may have remained in shock for a few days—like some of my students have—trying to make sense of you outperforming the friend you believed was smarter. And what about that friend's reaction? Did he accept that you were more proficient at that concept? Or did he react in a manner that you were unaccustomed to? Perhaps he gave you excuses on top of excuses as to why he didn't outperform you on that occasion.

For many people, getting good grades in a course means you're smart and very good at mastering that course; or that you can go to university to pursue studies in that subject area, and you will become successful. While for many, getting a low grade means you're not smart, or you're not good enough to do something. And if that thing is related to a field that you want to pursue, you're discouraged from pursuing it, and sometimes you're even told by your parents and teachers to pursue a career along the field where your marks are higher. While you may consider this to be great advice, do answer these questions: What percentage of the content you covered in high school have you been using in your everyday life? Take math for instance; what percentage of the math you learned in high school is applicable in your daily life, whether in your workplace or your personal day-to-day occurrences? Did you choose your career based on the subjects you excelled in, or based on what you genuinely like and wanted to pursue? And if you chose a career that was based solely on your grades, how are you liking your job? I believe it was Confucius who first said, *"Choose a job you love, and you will never have to work a day in your life."*

I believe getting good grades is significant for the following reasons:

- They motivate you to employ good work habits to maintain high marks.
- They make you feel very smart and intelligent.

- They help you to improve and maintain your self-esteem.
- They make your parents happy and proud of you.
- They put you in the cream of the crop for a program of study.

That said, the subject area you're doing well in is not necessarily your calling. Many people pursue studies in the areas where they excel the most, but later find themselves in jobs they do not like. Of course, they may be good at doing the job, but the self-fulfillment and daily motivation that they need, to wake up each morning and go to work, is just missing.

J.T. O'Donnell, founder and CEO of *Work It Daily*, who has been studying why people hate their jobs, for more than fifteen years now, says 70% of the workforce dislike their jobs, and this is because it's difficult for you to find a career path that makes you feel satisfied and truly successful. School doesn't teach you to find a career path, and grades don't dictate the appropriate career path for you. Finding the right career path is often very challenging and requires a lot of trial and error—failures and improvements—and this can make the journey daunting and discouraging. Michael Jordan missed thousands of baskets before he became the greatest basketball player of all time. The Wright brothers failed many times, and were even ridiculed and laughed at, before they got airplanes to fly; and Thomas Edison failed at the light bulb 10,000 times before he was successful. These are all examples of successful people who failed multiple times before they achieved greatness, yet school frown at failure.

So perhaps those courses that you liked but weren't so good at, just required more of your efforts and determination to perform better. Perhaps your gut was telling you that that's the path you wanted to travel, but your guidance counsellor encouraged you to take the easier path. Or maybe your parents discouraged you from becoming a musician because you had excellent science marks, and they wanted you to become a doctor. Perhaps you wanted to become an actor, but your parents said they saw the lawyer in you, and there's no actor in the family, so it's not in your genes. But while those good grades may cultivate many positives, they may be sending you the wrong message in terms of what's best for your ultimate success in life.

Passion and determination are great motivators to achieve success. This explains why this world has many successful college dropouts. They're not blindsided by grades or how well they did in school; they set their hearts on what drives them, what they want to achieve, and they take action. Thomas Edison said, *"I have not failed. I've just found 10,000 ways that won't work."* Successful people have positive attitudes; they embrace their fears and learn from their failures, focusing on perfecting one thing at a time while avoiding life's distractions. School doesn't teach you these things. In fact, school teaches you that failing is bad. Many teachers feel pressured to pass students who haven't satisfied the basic curriculum expectations, because if they have too many failures, they may be reprimanded. So, students are promoted from grade to grade, perpetually struggling at every level because the foundational skills were not acquired. When such students get into the real world and fail at something, do you think they will persevere, or will they give up quickly?

Is Failing Bad? What Grade Says You're Smart?

What do you think would have happened if you were able to choose the courses that you wanted to study, and you didn't have to write any tests or exams? Suppose you had to write evaluations, but you were never assigned a grade? Tests were just used to assess your progress, evaluate your learning, and tell you where you need to improve? Do you think you would have learned less? Do you think you would have been less smart than you are today? And what grade would you have been satisfied with in order to accept that you had learned the concepts taught? Would you have been okay with 60%, 70%, 80%, or 90%? Why did you choose that grade? Is that the grade that society uses to say that you are smart, or is that the grade that you believe is enough for you?

According to reports from The Guardian, at Oberländer's school, a school in Berlin, there are no timetables, no lecture-style instructions, and absolutely no grades until students turn 15. Students get to decide which subjects they want to study in a particular lesson, and when they want to write their exams. The school's headmaster, Margaret Rasfeld, contends that the philosophy behind their education reform is that the labour market is changing, and smartphones and the internet are transforming the way in which young people are processing information. The school has what they dubbed abstract courses like "responsibility" and "challenge." I don't believe these courses are really so abstract at all, because many students need to learn responsibility, how to take responsibility for their own learning, and how to challenge themselves to rise above mediocrity. Some students believe that teachers are responsible for their learning, and they blame their teachers whenever they fail, even when the data is glaring—showing that 98% of the other students in their class are passing, so there has to be more to a student failing than the teacher.

While I don't necessarily agree with all of Oberländer's philosophy, since I believe that not everyone is an independent, responsible, and self-reliant learner, or has the ability to excel with limited guidance, I do believe that setting higher expectations for students, and giving them some autonomy to make their own choices regularly, will see them excelling better. Much better than they do in an education system where decisions are mostly made for them, where they're compelled to do subjects that they have no interest in, or write evaluations that they are not ready for. Given more choices, students would ultimately choose what they prefer, and what motivates and interests them. I believe you will agree that many people achieve greater success in completing a milestone, when they enjoy whatever they're doing, or when they get the desired self-satisfaction when the task is completed. I believe it's worth quoting Confucius a second time: *"Choose a job you love, and you will never have to work a day in your life."*

I agree with Rasfeld that when you were a three or four-year-old child, you were full of self-confidence and couldn't wait to start school, but unfortunately, school somehow managed to deplete your wealth of confidence. Once you started attending school, you began to believe that failing is a bad thing. You no longer viewed failing as feedback to inform your future decisions and actions. Needing to try again—avoiding the mistakes you made before, like when you were learning to walk and kept falling—was no longer the lesson learned from failing. You started to view it as a label or even a character trait: *"I'm dumb. I'm not good at this or that. I'm just a complete failure. Why try when I know I'm going to fail anyway?"* These are some common sayings from my students. The mantra that *"no student gets left behind"* doesn't serve students well. It only limits some students' learning opportunities, because instead of giving them a second chance to learn and cement a concept that they struggle with properly, they are promoted from class to class, with gaps in their learning. By the time they get to high school, the gaps are so wide that some high school teachers have to dumb down the curriculum, which gives the false impression that some students are excelling.

In many ways, failing is considered the best feedback for everyone. You just need to examine why you failed, and identify strategies to improve your performance next time. And it's not just your failures that serve as feedback for you, but the failures of others too. In many self-help books, written by successful people, you will read about their failures and how they learned from them to move forward. The popular Post-it Notes that you use for sticky notes or bookmarks, were born from Dr. Spencer Silver's failure when he tried to develop a super strong adhesive. Arthur Fry saw the real usefulness of this failure when he needed a weak adhesive to anchor his bookmark in his hymn book, and that made Post-it Notes very popular today. I bet you can find a Post-it Note in your office or home right now. That shows that great successes can be born from embarrassing failures, and not necessarily from getting A^+ for completing a task.

Now that you know why good grades matter, and the effect that testing and grades have on your experience in school, you are ready to read the next chapter, which explores the high school math curriculum, its relevance to the career you choose, and how effective it is in preparing you for the real world.

2
The High School Math Curriculum

"Homework's hard. Especially math. My kids joke with me. They tell me they have homework. I say, 'Okay.' And then I sit down and they say, 'It's math.' 'No! Not math! English, history, anything!'"

—Angelina Jolie

How People View the Math Curriculum

Because Jamaica was last ruled by the British, its education system is based on Britain's. I started high school at grade 7, and completed in grade 13. When I finished grade 11, I was too young to attend university, so I opted to complete the additional two years (grades 12 and 13) offered at my high school. I completed high school in 1992. At the time of writing this chapter, it's three years shy of three decades ago. Over the past two decades, I have seen so many changes in the world and in how things are done, and yet the education system in Canada, a first world country, seems much the same as when I graduated then (in Jamaica, a third world country). Math and English are still the only two courses that are mandatory up to grade 11. Students are still studying Shakespeare in English, and most concepts taught in math are related to trigonometry and linear and quadratic functions.

Have you been in a conversation with someone you're meeting for the first time, and this question comes up: *What do you do for a living?* Have you ever felt like you're a superhuman after you share what you do? Let me share my experience with the career question. Whenever I'm asked the question, and I respond that I'm a teacher, the next two questions that follow are invariably related to what age group I teach—high school or elementary—and to the subjects that I teach.

The moment I share that I'm a math teacher, I get responses like: *"Oh, wow, you must be a brilliant lady. Math? I hated math; I just couldn't do it! Math was my worst subject in high school; I had nightmares before math tests."* And unfortunately, one that I hear regularly is: *"My teacher in grade 7 or grade 8 was so bad; after that class, I was turned off from math for life."* By the end of that segment of the conversation, I'm led to believe that math teachers have superior powers over other teachers. Do you know why people have this reaction?

What has bothered me over the years is: Why do I get the same reactions each time? And it's not just me; I've asked fellow math colleagues, and they too share similar experiences. Many of my students express similar sentiments from year to year, and they regularly ask: *"Ms., why do we have to do math? Why can't we just choose the subjects that we want to take?"* And some of my students have come to class with a preconceived perception that they will fail the course despite the efforts they make, so it makes no sense to even try or do any homework.

How about you? Did you have difficulty understanding mathematical concepts too? Was it your worst or your best subject? Did you like it so much that you spent more time doing it and paid less attention to other courses? If you're like me, who loved math and experienced lots of fun solving math problems, I know your other courses got less attention. Do you think people who love math and excel in it have a "math gene?" Gardner's theory of multiple intelligences proposes eight different intelligences, and logical-mathematical intelligence— number sense and reasoning smart—is one of the eight. Could it be that some people possess low logical-mathematical intelligence, and for this reason, find math difficult?

Many education policymakers contend that there's no "math gene," and that if the math curriculum is delivered the correct way, every student can learn. But what is the proper way? Perhaps mathematical success could be easily achieved if we could identify differentiated instruction that hit all or most of Gardner's eight types of intelligence, to deliver the math curriculum, but is it possible that there's a greater issue at hand—the curriculum itself? The current math curriculum may be too focused on abstract concepts that cannot be easily transformed into bodily-kinesthetic intelligence (body smart), musical intelligence (music smart), and naturalist intelligence (nature smart), for example.

Topics that are more applicable to real life, like those that focus more on household spending, planning for retirement and the science of money—how money is earned, invested, preserved, and multiplied, and how to make informed decisions about finances—would lend itself more to the different types of intelligence. However, the current math curriculum focuses too much on concepts such as geometry and functions that many students will not use in their jobs or daily activities. And for this reason, many of them believe the curriculum is old and outdated and not meeting their current needs, and therefore not providing the more useful skills that they will need in the future to achieve real-life success.

What Math Is Useful to Everyone?

You will agree that some careers need the abstract theoretical mathematical concepts that are in the current math curriculum. But is it necessary for all these concepts to be in all math courses, or should they be in optional ones, for students who wish to pursue these career paths to choose? The mandatory math courses should have more of the real-life concepts and skills that everyone uses in their daily lives. And what are these skills? Financial literacy skills. Students should be learning more about personal finance—good money sense; making informed decisions about budgeting, spending, investing for retirement, investing for their children's education, and using credit cards—than spending time covering multiple units on linear functions, geometry, quadratic functions, and trigonometry, which have little or no bearing on their lives now and in the future.

Over the years, I have seen students becoming increasingly disengaged in my math classes because they are becoming more aware and less gullible. With advanced technology, they can do the research themselves and determine what they will need, to pursue a career of their choice. They are catching on that my colleagues and I have been teaching them things that are hardly relevant to the career they want to pursue; hence, students' overall performance in math is declining. I cannot recycle some questions from tests I used five years ago, because they are too difficult for the current students. Consequently, my colleagues and I have to keep "dumbing down the tests" so to speak, so that current students can perform favourably. And this is happening in math courses at every level.

Even the overall performance in math, on the grade 6 and 9 standardized math assessment in Canada, for example, has been showing a downward trend in students' performance for the last few years. In an effort to improve results, the rules surrounding the test administration have been changing to give more leeway to students. For instance, every student is now allowed extra time—not just students with an individual learning plan—and resources are allowed on the walls, providing it meets specified criteria. The rationale is that these changes are geared towards making students feel more comfortable and have similar experiences during the standardized assessment, as they have during their class evaluations, but it is obvious that this is an attempt to boost declining performance. And while this will reduce some anxiety surrounding writing the standardized test, there is still a greater issue at hand: the curriculum itself. Even though changes to the guidelines may boost students' performance initially, I believe this is just a temporary fix. Replacing abstract concepts in the curriculum, with more practical ones, will promote and maintain higher students' performance in math, and in the standardized assessment by extension.

So, is it the current teaching strategies that are negatively impacting students' engagement and performance, or is it the irrelevant curriculum and the disconnection between the concepts taught and students' lived experiences? What if every math student is taught more practical concepts such as how to effectively save to accumulate an emergency fund, how to buy a home, how to lease or purchase a car, how to file their taxes, and how to save for their retirement and their children's education? Don't you think they would be more engaged in math classes? For example, consider a math project that requires students to research their expected income based on their career choice, then create a budget based on anticipated expenditures; then determine how long it would take them to save the down payment to purchase a car and a home; then determine what their monthly car payments and mortgage would be based on a certain interest rate, don't you think this would be extremely useful to them? Students would know before going in, whether their choice of career would give them the income and lifestyle they're anticipating. This would help them to make more practical career choices based on their findings, while weighing if it's worth pursuing studies in a particular field, and it could avoid them jumping from program to program— accumulating enormous student loan debt—when they get to college or university.

The Math Curriculum and the Real World

What percentage of the math concepts you covered in high school do you use in your daily life? How applicable is the math curriculum to the career that you chose to pursue? Did you learn the following topics in school?

- Money Sense and Spending Wisely
- Budgeting and Planning for Expenses
- Mortgages and Buying a Home

- Buying or Leasing a Car
- Saving for Your Children's Education
- Saving for Your Retirement
- Taxes and Tax Returns
- Assets and Liabilities
- Good Debt vs Bad Debt
- Saving and Investing
- Managing Credit Cards and Credit Scores

Do you think that these are topics that are applicable in your daily life and should be taught in school? And do you think that these topics should be covered in a separate course or that they could be integrated in the math curriculum? Compare those topics to the algebra, the functions, and the trigonometry and geometry that you learned in math. Do you think that these topics would have made your math courses appear less abstract? Do you think they would have been more interesting and engaging concepts, that make you hungry and want to learn more about these topics since they are a part of everyone's lived experiences?

While I agree that algebra, functions, trigonometry, and geometry have their place in the math curriculum, some of these concepts should be placed in optional math courses that students need for specific career paths. Some careers require only basic math skills, which students can acquire in well-designed courses to meet their needs. But forcing students to do math courses, with concepts that have no bearing on where they are heading, is wasting their time and not setting them up for real-life success. As a result, many students are demotivated, which leads to lower performances. This, of course, kills their self-esteem and makes them feel like they're not smart enough because they cannot do the math, which sometimes indirectly affects their performances in other courses, and thus gives a false impression of their true potential.

Is the Math Curriculum Changing to Match the Real world?

The math curriculum that I'm currently teaching has pretty much been around since 2002, and in many ways, it appears to be the same curriculum I covered when I was in high school. The few changes that were made to the curriculum since then were more about deleting things or focusing on the more simplified aspects of some concepts. Nothing was really changed or added to reflect the many changes in the real world since 2002. For instance, only a few of us still use a travel agency to book our airline tickets and cruises, and many people are moving away from a landline phone—some millennials have no concept of a landline. Some of us no longer take taxis but use Uber or Lyft to get to our destination. All our smartphones come with calculators, and applications like Mathway, Photomath, and Papa Math, which can manipulate fractions and integers, solve algebra problems, graph functions, and much more. If there weren't a cheating issue surrounding cellphones, which causes teachers to ban their usage during evaluations, some students would no longer purchase a calculator.

Don't you think it is ample time for a change? And don't get me wrong; I believe every student should acquire the essential math skills that are needed to function in everyday life, but the depth of the math courses they pursue should be either relevant to their career path or to the real world. Studying some mathematical concepts should be optional for students, especially for those who do not wish to pursue math at a postsecondary level. Some mathematical concepts are gruelling for many students and can cause severe stress and anxiety. Consequently, some students become disengaged—sometimes even depressed— when they are struggling in a math course. Others may even develop low self-esteem and self-worth, and believe that they are not smart, just because they have difficulties mastering a single subject. Unfortunately, this is a result of the high importance parents and society in general put on math performance because sadly, many people believe that a student with high math grades is smarter than their counterparts.

Which Professions Need Intense Math?

During my research, some of the careers I came across that require deeper math are:

1. Math Teachers and Professors
2. Actuaries
3. Computer Scientists and Designers
4. Computer Games Designers
5. Scientists and Forensic Scientists
6. Astronauts
7. Statisticians and Mathematicians
8. Engineers and Architects
9. Financial Advisors and Economists
10. Healthcare Professionals

I was, however, curious about how much of the math that was studied in high school or university, was used by people in these professions in their daily lives, so I interviewed a few of them. The question I asked was: *What percentage of the math you learned in high school and university, do you use in your career and daily life?* Here are the responses I received from people in the different professions. The responses are mostly verbatim. I only omitted comments that didn't add anything to what I kept, beyond emphasizing why the stated percentage is more likely correct or may even be overstated.

The Doctor: "I would say I use 2%, more or less."

The Nurse: "I think I use about 20% … For drug calculations, it's computed by the pharmacy, so I do use a small bit."

The Engineer: "I would say around 20%, and that may even be too high."

The Accountant: "I'm not sure what percentage to put on that, but I would say I mostly use more of the basics, like tables, addition, subtraction, division, multiplication, and integers. Other areas such as algebra, geometry, and trigonometry, not so much."

The Dentist: "In dental school, there was no math per say, but there was a lot of graphics, probability, and physical and materials science that drew heavily on mathematical concepts learned.

"And now, in my day-to-day 'chairside' dental practice, I use very little math in my procedures; but I still need to make important calculations about financial estimates, and rely on my math background to interpret a great deal of graphic representation when studying new procedures.

"So, I would say I use math in less than 10% of my day-to-day life. But understanding the basic principles of math has been essential for my training and ultimate success."

The Actuary: "Not as much as you might think—the more senior one gets in this profession, the less math you use. It's much more about managing internal and external relationships; however, I'd say that theory of interest and life contingencies are ever present, probably underlying 50% to 75% of our work, but personally, these days, I might be exposed to only about 25% of the math I learned."

The Software Engineer: "I use very little math—less than 10%. Perhaps only 5%, because with smartphones and computers, everything is easily available. The little math I use, I think I learned that before high school. But I loved high school math; I believe it helped me to be able to problem-solve and critically analyze things better."

When I asked the software engineer if his problem solving and critical and analytical skills would be less developed if high school math had more real-life scenarios to problem solve—such as determining if a family can afford to purchase a home at a certain price point, based on their income, expenses, and savings—he hastened to say that situations like those would have certainly been more useful than some of the abstract topics that were covered. He also shared that some of the math courses are definitely more suitable for stronger math students, and students who wish to pursue certain careers. He explained why he thinks some topics, like algebra and trigonometry, can turn off some students.

I don't think I need to say anymore for this section. I'll leave you to judge how much of the math you learned in school is applicable in a profession and to people's lives, based on the earlier responses given.

Why Is Math a Prerequisite?

None of the professionals I interviewed for the previous section said they used even one-quarter of the math that they studied in high school. The dentist, for instance, said he didn't do a lot of math in dental school. And I believe the concepts like probability and graphs, to name a few that he mentioned, are concepts that can be easily covered and mastered in dental school. So, if the percentage of math used in these professions is so low, why do we place so much emphasis on math in schools, and why is math a major prerequisite for these professions that—quote, unquote—required higher-level math courses?

I believe there are students who have lower math skills who could excel in some of the professions that require a math prerequisite course with a high mark. But these students may never know, because they weren't given the opportunity to pursue such careers, due to their lower performance in the subject. Students' dreams are often shattered because of the barriers created by program prerequisite courses. Some students are accepted into universities but are later told they cannot pursue a particular program because their math mark wasn't high enough. For this reason, they felt compelled to pursue studies in a program that doesn't match their dreams and aspirations. This sometimes results in students moving from program to program, digging deeper and deeper into student loan debt. And in some cases, at the end of their university career, they have a bachelors in a field that doesn't even interest them, or they can't find gainful employment in that field of study. Brian Tracy, in his book, *The Science of Money*, said 80% of college students never work in their field of major because the courses that they pursue are useless. Instead of taking courses to increase their earning ability, they pursue courses that often leave them unemployable after graduation.

Sometimes they end up searching for jobs they don't want, in fields they don't even like, just because that's the credentials they have to show. This often leads to job dissatisfaction and sometimes depression, and now suicide is becoming a growing problem in some universities. I believe this can be avoided, because passion and motivation are characteristics that many people will demonstrate if achieving their goals is at stake. A student who underperforms in math in high school doesn't automatically translate to poor performance in math in college and university. I have seen students perform poorly in grade 9 math, but by the time they enter grade 12, their performance improves immensely, due to maturity and the determination to achieve acceptance in their desired program of study.

The question still remains, however: If so little math is used in the workplace and in people's daily lives, why is high school math mandatory for every student up to grade 11? And why is a high math mark one of the prerequisites for certain professions? Is it that the math is needed for the university programs, or is it a case that universities judge students' abilities according to their math grade? Is it possible that universities think that only students with high math scores are capable of performing well in programs like engineering and forensic science, for example? It would be interesting to see the performance data, if students with low math marks, who have a strong interest in these fields, are allowed to pursue them. Join me in the next chapter, where I will share my experience as a math teacher in the classroom, and explain why more and more students are becoming increasingly disengaged in math classes, and why less aspiring teachers are pursuing math in teachers college.

3

My Experience as a Math Teacher

"I'm not much of a math and science guy. I spent most of my time in school daydreaming, and managed to turn it into a living.

—George Lucas

Why Students Are Disengaged

Engaging students can be very challenging and even frustrating for teachers in some subject areas, and I believe it is especially true for mathematics teachers. A Gallup study, done in 2012, which surveyed half a million students in 37 states in America, reported that about 24% of fifth graders, 39% of middle schoolers, and 56% of high school students are disengaged. I found this study alarming because I actually thought students would become more engaged as they became more mature. I thought students would no longer view the world as a playground for playing and having fun, but as a place to obtain an education to put them in a better position to get a job in the future, to care for themselves and their families. I tried to find a similar study that is focused on just math, but wasn't successful. Gallup identifies potential causes for disengagement, such as standardized testing, the failure to promote entrepreneurial skills, and curricula that lack pathways for students who will not, and do not want to, go to college or university.

As a math teacher, over the years, I've gotten the popular question: *"Ms., why do we need to learn this?"* and the sister one, *"When will we use this in the real world?"* Now a third question is becoming popular: *"Ms., who in their right mind actually uses this in the real world?"* Students are becoming more perceptive and are looking for relevance in what we are teaching them. And their thinking is obviously in line with what is evident in the real world, because as I've mentioned in the previous chapter, none of the employees I interviewed in the various professions use even one-quarter of the math they studied in high school or university. And all those professions required a high math mark in calculus or advanced functions to pursue studies in those areas.

Studies have shown that over the past decade, there's a reduction in the number of math teachers who majored in math at university. Many of them didn't even do a minor in math because they thought it was too difficult—it was easier to take math as an additional qualification. Some of my colleagues shared that they took math as an additional qualification because it's good to have math as a teachable, since more math jobs are available, and because math is mandatory for students up to grade 11. I don't think this trend will change, because many students, in Toronto for example, who require a high mark in calculus and/or advanced functions to study a desired program at university, are resorting to taking these courses at night school or private schools. The rationale is that night school is easier than day school because there isn't enough time to complete some topics, and they are pretty much guaranteed a high mark in private school since they are paying for the course, and their teachers are pressured to give higher marks if they want to keep their jobs. As a result, there has been a decrease in the number of high school students studying advanced math in day school. There is no doubt a correlation between fewer teachers majoring in math, and the reduction in students studying math in day school. If less students are studying advanced math the traditional way, this will inevitably lead to fewer young math teachers majoring in mathematics.

What is causing this trend?

A number of factors could be responsible for this, but here is a list of things that I believe are responsible:

- Students' attitudes and personal skills
- Students' experiences at school and home
- The distraction from social media and video games
- Outdated and irrelevant curriculum that shows very little applicability in the real-world

- A lack of skilled math teachers at the elementary level to give students a strong math foundation
- Inadequate teacher training to keep up with the changing world and students' diverse learning styles
- Pedagogical practices that are disconnected from students' interaction in the digital age

In Canada, for example, it is the less qualified math teachers who commonly teach math in elementary schools, or math at the lower level in the high schools. And many of these teachers are not trained adequately to perpetuate an engaging math classroom. Remember how I mentioned before that one of the common comments I get whenever I share that I'm a math teacher, is that their elementary teacher turned them off from math? Well, this explains why. And no blame to the elementary teachers; teachers shouldn't be expected to teach what they themselves do not know. I'm always in awe of elementary teachers because they usually teach students most subjects. My elementary school went from grade one to six, and my elementary teacher, in each grade, taught me every subject. My grandfather had a saying: *"If you're a jack of all trades, you're a master of none,"* which essentially means that if you're dabbling in everything, then you will not become a master of anything. Imagine elementary school teachers who weren't strong in math. Do you think such teachers would easily become master math teachers? Or would they more likely gain mastery in the subject areas that they excelled in?

And yet I believe if the math curriculum was more applicable and relevant to not just students but teachers as well, lending itself to more real-life application concepts, it would be easier for math teachers in general to improve their self-efficacy in mathematics. And why? Because what they are teaching would be so applicable to their own lived experiences, and they would have more stories to share, and more real-life examples to work through. They could use their personal situations to help students problem-solve scenarios. But instead, they are tasked with delivering a more abstract curriculum, with very few topics with which they can use their own experiences to teach.

A more relevant curriculum would prove more engaging for both teachers and students, and the learning environment would be more practical and meaningful. Teaching and learning are easier for everyone when there is a direct connection between what is being taught and learned, and people's views of the world or what they can identify with. A curriculum that involves more problem solving of real-life scenarios would be easier for teachers to deliver. That would no doubt engage teachers more, and students' engagement will likely increase since students often emulate the attitude of their teachers in a classroom.

Why Many Students Struggle with Math

Throughout my teaching career, I have spent many evenings while driving home, and many nights while marking, asking myself: *"Why is Tom still having difficulty understanding this concept? Why couldn't Nira solve this problem, when we did a few questions like this in the review the day before? Why didn't Amrit get that question when he asked me to do the same one the day before the test?"* This questioning session usually ends with: *"What am I not doing right? What can I do differently?"*

These questions have helped to guide my teaching practice over the years. I've learned to utilize differentiated instruction, technology-based instructions, and the Universal Design for Learning— an instructional strategy that gives every student an equal opportunity to succeed—to improve my pedagogy. I've also implemented various unique strategies and methodologies that I gleaned from multiple colleagues over the years, to help students overcome specific challenges in understanding some mathematical concepts. And for the first ten years of my career, I seemed to have it all under control, until I got a grade 10 essential math class for the first time. I believe, before that year, I would have been grossly incorrect if I said I knew how to teach math at every level.

For perspective, I started my teaching career teaching math at the advanced level. For those of you who know about the GCE A Level exams—written in England and administered to students in many British colonies at the time—and the CAPE exams—developed to phase out the A Level exams for Caribbean students, because it was believed to be too culturally biased—you will understand that my clientele would have been students who were strong in math. Only high performing math students would pursue math courses at those levels. When I came to Canada, I was tasked with teaching math courses at the advanced and general levels, and soon after, the academic and applied level. With some adjustments to my pedagogical approach, and my collaboration with colleagues, things were panning out just fine, until I got my first essential class.

It was a class of 10 students according to the roster, but only seven showed up the first few days—and often not the same seven either. That was the first time I was in a class where 100% of the students didn't want to be there. Every student in that class believed they were being forced to do a course they had no interest in, and they felt positive there was absolutely no way I could change their thinking.

That year, my learning curve increased exponentially on many fronts. From those students, I gathered some reasons as to why students struggled in math. Most of these reasons kept recurring over the years, and my list has been growing. Here are some of the reasons I have:

- Poor math foundation
- Poor retention
- Self-fulfilling prophecy
- The inability to relate learning to experience
- The fear of being wrong
- Insufficient time to process one concept before having to move on to another
- Too many abstract topics unrelated to lived experience
- Boring problem-solving processes
- Too many formulas to remember
- A negative preconception of self
- Parents perception of math
- Math test anxiety
- Dyscalculia

I have dyscalculia listed last, because this is something I've picked up on in more recent years. Dyscalculia is like dyslexia but is related to numbers and math. It's a condition that causes students to struggle in several areas relating to mathematics, like reading numbers correctly, using formulas properly, labeling shapes appropriately, and understanding and processing math problems accurately. This became apparent to me one year, when one of my students would always say the number correctly but would write it incorrectly. While the digits written were usually correct, they were often written in the wrong order, or a six may be written for a nine, and vice versa.

Back to My Essential Math Class

In the first week of class, I started to feel that students were correct about my inability to motivate them to learn. What saved me, however, were the real-life application topics to be covered—topics such as Spending Money, Working for Money, and Planning a Trip. The first topic we covered was Spending Money, and this made all the difference. I could easily tell stories and use examples from my lived experience, and cite simple real-life problems, while drawing on students' experiences that we could logically solve together. That created a shift in my students' paradigm, and caused them to relent on their perception about the course. They became motivated to learn, and eventually, I had seven regular attendees. They were interested in the financial education I taught them, because they could relate to it, it made sense to them, and they wanted to learn more. But their motivation evidently reduced when we were covering a unit like measurement, for instance, that didn't relate much to money. The part of the measurement unit that interested them the most was where they were required to design their bedroom or their ideal bedroom, and determine how much it would cost to furnish it and paint the room, based on wall measurements and given paint cost.

Evidently, this showed that students were more engaged when money was involved in their learning, and when they could make the connection between what they were learning and their real lives. Later, when the roster was reduced to 8 students, many days I had 100% attendance, even though one of them refused to show up on evaluation days. In the end, only that one student failed, and I believed he could have also passed if he wasn't adamant about skipping tests and his summative evaluation. The lesson here is, if you make the teaching and content relevant, students will show up to learn; focusing on a topic like money evidently motivated students to engage and participate in the learning environment.

The Greatest Barriers for Math Learners

Because the math curriculum is highly sequential and progressive—fundamental concepts must be learned successfully before you can move on to other concepts—math learners often become confused, lost, or feel disempowered to achieve success in this subject. Students who have difficulties in other courses may even experience more dissonance when learning mathematical concepts, because trying to learn the math procedures and achieving logical understanding simultaneously, can increase anxiety and become daunting. The challenges that students experience in learning math should be labelled as barriers, which if overcome, could perhaps lead to a higher success rate in math performance. But what are some of these barriers?

The Vocabulary

Reading and understanding the language of mathematics can be challenging because some words are not used in your daily vernacular. There are many words, such as numerator, perpendicular, tangent, hypotenuse, reciprocal, and discriminant, which are used only in mathematics. These words are not familiar to students until they learn them in math courses, and they often forget them because they're not used regularly in their daily communications. Plus, some words have a different meaning in the language of mathematics than they have in the English language. These include words such as roots, mean, zeros, product, odd, and square.

The Syntax

Many students have difficulty understanding the syntax that is used in mathematics because it is more complex and very different from what they are accustomed to. For instance, consider the two syntaxes:

1. *The base of a rectangle is 5 less than twice the width,*
2. *The sum of twice the square of a number, and triple the square of another number, is forty-one.*

Now, pause and write down the equations to represent what you just read. Reread if necessary. How many times did you read before you understood what each statement was saying? Were you able to write two equations, and how confident are you that those equations are correct? Time to check your answers:

Equation 1: $b = 2w - 5$, where b represents the base and w the width.

Equation 2: $2x^2 + 3y^2 = 41$, where x and y are the numbers.

Were you correct? Congratulations if you were!

The Formulas

Memorizing mathematical formulas is very challenging for many students because they cannot identify a connection between what they are memorizing and their lived experiences. But memorizing is not the only problem. Recognizing when to select the appropriate formula to solve a given problem may not be easily identifiable for some students. Some students are successful in memorizing the formulas but, on the other hand, have no idea when to use them. Other students know which formula would be applicable in a certain situation but have difficulty recalling the formula. Do you remember the formula for the Pythagorean Theorem? And what about the Quadratic Formula to determine the roots of a quadratic equation? If you left school several years ago, the term *"roots of a quadratic equation"* may even sound very foreign to you now.

The Problem-Solving Process

Many mathematical processes involve multiple steps that must be executed in a specified order. If the correct order is not employed, the final result will be incorrect. Many students do not spend time reading the instructions, and some have difficulty reading and understanding what the problem is asking. Some may even read part of the problem and assume or anticipate what the question should be asking. For this reason, they don't take the time to work through the problem appropriately before starting to work on it, and they may miss key information that is required to obtain the correct solution. And there are those students who do understand the problem but have challenges remembering the correct steps to solve it or the correct formula that is required to complete certain steps. This often leads to dissonance and frustration, so some students associate the problem-solving process with anxiety and exasperation, and completely avoid it instead of embracing it.

Learning Gaps

Because most elementary schools do not have specialized subject teachers, many students have learning gaps when they enter high school. And the learning gaps in math always seem to be the greatest. It is no fault of the elementary teachers because, as mentioned before, teachers cannot teach what they themselves do not know or are not comfortable teaching. An elementary teacher who is required to teach most subjects to their students, will rarely achieve mastery in all the subject areas. And math is perhaps the most disliked subject among elementary school teachers. The next time you meet an elementary teacher or talk to your child's elementary teacher, ask which subject is the least preferred to teach.

Irrelevant Curriculum

Relating the math curriculum to the real world is a challenge that not only students face but teachers as well. There are many topics, such as measurement, ratio, proportion, and percentage, which can be easily related to the real world, but there are also many topics, like algebra, exponents, square roots, and polynomial functions, which are not as relatable. These topics are very foreign to students, and they don't see them in their daily lives; therefore, they have difficulty making the connection and seeing their relevance in the real world. Topics relating to money, budgeting, saving, spending, investing, saving on taxes, and other concepts to do with personal finance, would create less barrier to learning for math learners at every level. Why? Because these are concepts relating to money that students can easily recognized are very relevant to them.

Challenges in the Math Classroom

Teachers and students, in general, face many challenges in the classroom. However, the problems experienced are even more exacerbated for math teachers and math learners. While many of the challenges may be teacher and student centered, some are systemic that teachers have no control over. I will discuss some of these challenges and how even minor changes could help to reduce some of them.

Large Class Size

I always find it mind-boggling that math is one of the most challenging subjects for many students, yet math classes have the largest class size. A typical grade 9 and 10 academic math class, in the Toronto District School Board, will have anywhere from 28 to 32 students. A teacher usually feels very lucky if he has less than 30 students in these courses. For simplicity, let's consider a grade 9 academic class of 30 students. A typical period for grade 9 students is 75 minutes. If the teacher uses 10 minutes to interact with students, set the stage for the lesson, and complete the attendance, then 20 minutes to complete and consolidate an activity, and 30 minutes to complete concrete concepts and examples in the lesson, only 15 minutes are remaining in the period. That is only enough time to spend 30 seconds, one-on-one, helping each student. And you may be saying that not every student needs one-on-one help, which I totally agree with. But what about the five students who may need more than 3 minutes, one-on-one, to complete a question or an exit ticket to get some feedback? Where is the time to check-in and provide feedback to the other 25 students?

Teacher Training

I went to teachers' college more than 20 years ago, and it's even longer for some of my colleagues. Google Classroom, BrightSpace, YouTube, smartphones, tablets, and many software applications, like Desmos,

Photomath, and Mathway, never existed at the time. Hence, the teacher training I received was from a different era. So many things have changed since, including how students learn, yet the ongoing training that my school board should be providing, so that teachers can keep up with the changing times, is extremely limited. We have very few professional development sessions throughout the year, and most times, the agendas for these sessions do not include any hands-on teacher training. At most of the professional development sessions, I only have people talking at me—saying what I should be doing but not showing me how to do it. Luckily for me, I'm very tech-savvy—computer science is my second teachable—and I can embark on self-directed learning activities to keep up with teaching strategies in the twenty-first century. But what about my colleagues who aren't tech-savvy, and dislike computers; how can they keep up with the changing times when they're not receiving hands-on training? Sometimes I do wonder if those keynote speakers at the professional development sessions, who don't give tangible examples of what they are saying, can actually demonstrate how to implement their suggestions in the classroom.

Students' Disengagement

Despite the efforts my colleagues and I have been making to teach math using twenty-first-century strategies, making it culturally relevant, free from oppressive barriers, and pulling on examples from students' lived experiences, I still see more and more students becoming disengaged in my math classes. Invariably, the students who remain very motivated are the ones who plan to pursue careers such as engineering and computer science, which require a high math mark for college programs. And even the students who are strong in math, but do not wish to pursue studies in programs that need math, show limited interest because they can't see any longterm benefit.

How Can the Math Curriculum Be More Relevant?

What is mathematics? I typed in this question in Google, and here are a few examples of what the search returned:

1. *Mathematics is the abstract science of number, quantity, and space.*
2. *Mathematics is the science that deals with the logic of shape, quantity, and arrangement.*
3. *The four thinking math standards are problem-solving, communication, reasoning, and connections. It is not about answers; it's about processes.*
4. *Mathematics is an aid to representing and attempting to resolve problem situations in all disciplines. It is an interdisciplinary tool and language.*
5. *Math is all around us, in everything we do. It is the building block for everything in our daily lives, including mobile devices, architecture (ancient and modern), art, money, engineering, and even sports.*

Number five stood out the most for me because I believe it to be true. Math is all around us, and it is an integral part of many things that we do daily. However, I don't believe the high school math curriculum, especially at the academic and university level, effectively portrays math as a building block for everything around us. I didn't have that perception as a student, and I don't believe teachers are adequately trained to view it as such, at least not in my time. Yes, I was told that math is in many things around us, and some real examples were given where math is used in the real world. Still, the actual work done during class focused more on computations, graphing, remembering and applying formulas, solving equations, knowing the set of rules to solve various problems, verifying conjectures, and proving that a mathematical statement is true.

In an article by Dr. Robert H. Lewis, professor of Mathematics at Fordham University, he cited that there is a great misconception about mathematics; that it is an *"unconsciously held delusion that mathematics is a set of rules and formulas that have been worked out by god knows who for god knows why."* I wasn't surprised to read that, because chances are I would have had the same delusion if I hadn't been a math teacher for so many years. It was only with the advent of technology, and being able to research and watch videos of how math instructions can include more culturally relevant things and more real-life application phenomena, that my perception changed.

In the previous section, where I shared about how I got my students in my first essential math class to become motivated and more engaged in learning math, I cited how their interest peaked when the topics were related to money and real-life experiences. My experience over the years is that every student—not just those in essential math—love to explore and learn about things relating to money and finances. Even students who have an interest in pursuing programs in the STEM field, which require higher-level math, become very engaged when the topic of money comes up. What causes this? It's because money is related to pretty much everything we do in our lives, and everyone knows they will need money for even basic survival needs. So it makes sense that everyone would pay attention to what they need to possess for their ultimate survival.

Hence, if math is the building block for everything in our lives, and money is such an essential thing that everyone uses every day in real life, shouldn't money be an integral part of every math curriculum? Not everyone is into mobile devices, architecture, art, engineering, or sports, but everyone is into money. So why are there three chapters on quadratic relations, and two chapters on trigonometry, in the most recently published grade 10 academic textbook used in Canada, while there is no chapter on money? Wouldn't it make more sense to have five chapters on concepts relating to money? Better yet, on financial literacy on a broad scope?

And I'm not saying that quadratic relations and trigonometry are not useful for some disciplines, but I believe more focus should be placed on what is more beneficial to the masses, and on what everyone will definitely need and utilize. A math curriculum that is beneficial, meaningful, and relevant to students' lived experiences, now and in the future, is more suitable for them to learn. The earlier children are exposed to the science of money and financial education, the higher the possibility of them becoming financially successful. Every high school math curriculum should cover the following topics:

- Money Sense and Spending Wisely
- Budgeting and Planning for Expenses
- Mortgages and Buying a Home
- Buying or Leasing a Car
- Saving for Education and Retirement
- Taxes and Tax Returns
- Assets and Liabilities
- Good Debt vs Bad Debt
- Saving and Investing
- Managing Credit Cards and Credit Scores
- Insurance and Asset Protection
- Business and Entrepreneurship

And it shouldn't matter if students are pursuing math at the essential, applied, academic, college, or university level. No student should complete high school without learning about these concepts. The onus would be on the teacher to plan instructions that fit within the learning culture, the learning styles, and the interests of the students they have in front of them. Demonstrating a certain level of knowledge in financial literacy should be just as important as showing a certain level of expertise in numeracy and English literacy, to obtain a high school diploma. So, the math curriculum should place a greater focus on the science of money and financial education, than on algebra and geometry, which many students deem useless, because they will never use them after they leave high school.

Should High School Math Be Optional?

I believe every high school student should learn mathematics, because it triggers the rational part of their thinking, and it also helps to increase the logical ability of every student. Moreover, it helps them to make connections and improve their problem solving, communication, and reasoning with justification skills. But what remains questionable, however, are some of the topics that are taught in the high school math curriculum. Would you say the math curriculum is meeting students' needs at the grade and content level? Do a mental reflection, and identify which of the following topics you find useful in your daily life.

- Algebra and Polynomials
- Linear Systems and Equations
- Measurement and Geometry
- Trigonometry

- Linear and Quadratic Relations
- Transformation of Functions
- Exponential and Logarithmic Functions

While I am confident that these topics help to improve your problem-solving skills, push you to think critically, and increase your logical reasoning ability, most of the math that you use after leaving school is definitely fundamental. And this level of math could have been attained without having to cover those challenging concepts that have no bearing on your career or future dealings. There are many real-life application topics that involve mathematics, which can be used to improve everyone's problem-solving, logical reasoning, and critical thinking skills.

Most of the topics listed above are the ones that you or your friends may have struggled with, and had no interest in learning. You and your classmates may have become disengaged when learning them, thus defeating the purpose of learning math to increase your analytical and logical thinking. And perhaps those were the same ones you found most abstract, and you couldn't relate them to your lived experiences. Hence, they created a disconnect from your reality. But what if your math courses had focused more on creating a budget, based on given earnings and expenses, identifying strategies to cut costs and increase savings, and investing wisely for your children's education and your own retirement? Do you think you would have struggled the same? Do you think that would have been more useful to you than being asked to determine the values for x and y that would make an equation true?

The mandatory math courses should serve your needs now and later in your life. They should focus more on money and financial literacy. You should not be compelled to learn things that frustrate and create anxiety for you and fellow learners. This may have even mitigated against you performing optimally in the other courses that interest you more, because the time and effort spent labouring over confusing math problems could have been channeled to other courses. You should be given the opportunity to choose the math courses that have topics that you want to learn and find interesting, or ones that will be useful for your future career. And even if you found some topics very easy but have no intention to pursue careers that require them, you shouldn't be forced to complete those courses either, since they are of no use to you later. Although the education system varies from country to country, there are stark similarities in many countries. I believe the traditional education system that is common around the world, covers too much irrelevant content, and it causes students and teachers unnecessary stress and frustration in some subject areas—math especially.

In many ways, the curriculum objectives and expectations ultimately waste your time, because you could use the time that is spent learning irrelevant concepts, to cover topics that are more relevant to your interest or career path. Or you could use that time to acquire skills that you will need to function effectively and become a more responsible citizen in society. Ultimately, you should be given the choice to choose whether you want to pursue a particular math course at a certain grade level; you shouldn't be compelled to pursue a course you dislike or struggle with. Now read on to learn what is definitely missing from the high school curriculum, and could be easily integrated into every course, especially the math ones, to make them more engaging and applicable to your lived experiences, and which you could use to conduct your everyday activities in the future.

4
Financial Literacy Is Missing

"School systems should base their curriculum not on the idea of separate subjects, but on the much more fertile idea of disciplines... which makes possible a fluid and dynamic curriculum that is interdisciplinary."

—Ken Robinson

The School Curriculum Needs Overhauling

Where are you in your life? Perhaps you already completed your studies, got your dream job, and are enjoying life with your family, on your terms. Maybe you're still studying and wondering if you will get that dream job at the end of your academic career and be very successful. Perhaps you don't have or want a job, or you are self-employed, or you want to be your own boss. Wherever you are in the stage of your life, and knowing what you already know, I would like to ask you a series of questions:

- Do you like your high school curriculum?
- What part of the curriculum do you consider to be most beneficial?
- What aspects of the curriculum do you deem irrelevant to your lived experiences?
- Are there things you believe are missing from the curriculum that you think would have been more beneficial?
- If you think that things are missing from the curriculum, what are they?
- What is your idea of an ideal high school curriculum?

In the 2014/2015 school year, I started to do a simple survey with my students at the end of each semester; I call it the *Start Stop Continue Survey*. I got the idea from my then principal, Valerie Nelson, who was a great proponent of giving students and teachers a voice. Primarily, students would share what they disliked throughout the course and wanted to stop, what they loved and wanted to see continue, and the things that they would have loved to see or experience—but never did—and would like to start experiencing. You may consider the above questions as part of the *Start Stop Continue Survey,* in relation to the school curriculum.

My ideal school curriculum is one that gives you choices to pursue what interests you the most, one that equips you with the necessary skills to engage in healthy habits, to effectively conduct your daily affairs, and to cultivate global competencies in all facets of your life. These are the skills to build and maintain good and healthy relationships; to love and care for others despite their gender, race, or sexual preferences; to be independent, ambitious, and responsible, and to make good decisions when it comes to your health and finances, to name a few. Having the skills to effectively conduct your financial affairs, heavily impacts your health, your lifestyle, and your well-being, before and after retirement. Many high-income earners are drowning in debt and living from paycheck to paycheck. If they are not paid for a month or two, they are in deep, deep, you know what, and the probability that they will become bankrupt is a high percentage. Many marriages also fail because of financial dilemmas stemming from irresponsible spending. Why do you think this occurs?

There's an old adage that says, *"A fool and his money will soon be parted."* And I believe this is where the education system is failing young people. Our education system focuses too much on training you to become cogs in a machine. It teaches you to become employees who work for money instead of teaching you how to have money working for you. Many students leave school believing they have limited potential and cannot achieve greatness because they "fail to conform" to a predefined education system that wasn't designed for modern-day students. The system also limits your choices; it teaches you that success can only be had if you make the grades that society dubbed as favourable. Additionally, it makes you believe that failing is a bad thing; and for this reason, you spend your life trying not to fail, instead of accepting that failing creates more opportunities to learn, and the key is to learn from your failures.

What is rather ironic is that although school grooms you to become an employee to work for money, it doesn't equip you with the necessary skills to make smart choices when it comes to money. Even those students who take optional business courses that have elements of financial literacy embedded in the curriculum, know very little about the science of money. And I don't believe this is any fault of these students or their teachers. The system itself causes students to focus more on getting a grade on their report card that is pleasing to the eyes, than on learning essential skills to become financially successful. Not only that, because the importance of financial literacy skills is not stressed in schools—and is not a part of the school culture—small doses of it here and there is inadequate to effect long-term change in business students. If the science of how to save, spend, and invest money, how it can be multiplied, how you can preserve it, and how you can have it working for you, was covered in all the school curricula, students would catch on, and the importance of financial literacy would become the culture of every school.

With new advancements in technology, and the advent of artificial intelligence, more and more jobs are being done by robots instead of by humans. Many companies are moving jobs overseas because it is cheaper to pay workers in China, India, and the Philippines, for instance, than it is to pay workers in countries like America and Canada. Also, more companies are increasingly investing in automated systems. Just step into a MacDonald's, a Walmart, or a movie theater in some cities, and you'll see more self-checkout stations than you see cashiers.

What is the implication here? The workforce is slowly shrinking, year after year. Consequently, our education system may be setting you up for more failure than success. Reports show that more than 50% of Americans leaving high school are illiterate and cannot fill out a job application form. So, it appears that schools may not even be meeting students' needs where English literacy is concerned. Other reports also show that more than 50% of college students in America remain unemployed for more than a year after graduation, and some of those employed have to take menial jobs that are not related to their field of study. Although I couldn't find similar reports for Canada, I have no doubt the situation is very much the same for Canadians because I've heard complaints from some of my past students. Hence, it seems it's not just the school curriculum in our countries that need some overhauling to keep up with imparting the knowledge and skills that students need to function effectively in society, our post-secondary institutions also need some work in that area.

Why Financial Literacy Should Be Included

Everyone needs to have good money sense and know how to manage their money to achieve financial independence. Have you ever wondered why many lottery winners end up broke after a few years, or why many professional athletes, who earned millions in the peak of their career, end up broke shortly after their careers end? Sammy Davis Jr. said: *"Ten million dollars after I'd become a star, I was deeply in debt."* I will reiterate the saying: *"A fool and his money will soon be parted."* Without financial education, it doesn't matter how much money some people earn; they will blow it all in a short time. Financial literacy impacts the way people spend, save, borrow, invest, and manage their financial affairs.

Atkinson and Messy define financial literacy as a combination of awareness, knowledge, skill, attitude, and behavior necessary to make sound financial decisions and ultimately achieve individual well-being. In order to increase your financial literacy skills, financial education should be an integral part of your education program. It should start at the elementary level, and each year of schooling, you should build on previous knowledge, learning age-appropriate concepts relating to good money sense. This would equip you with the set of skills and knowledge that allows you to make informed and effective decisions, based on how money works in the world, how you can make more of it, how you manage it, how you invest it or turn it into more, and how you may donate it to help others.

Many Canadians and Americans are unprepared for major life events such as retirement, college education, purchasing a home, and an unexpected event such as the death or unemployment of a spouse who is the breadwinner of the family. The Canadian Payroll Association (CPA) sixth annual survey of thousands of Canadian employees, conducted in 2014, found that more Canadians are living paycheque to paycheque, and most are saving less than they should for meeting their retirement goals. The CPA also reported that debt was a primary concern of participants in the survey, as 39% of employees shared that they felt overwhelmed by their level of debt. This represented a 7% increase over what the association had found in the previous two years. To make matters worse, some participants believe they will never be debt-free. No doubt poor spending attitude, low savings rates, and high consumer debt are putting financial strains on many families and the economy. As academia Edward Taylor and Karin Forte put it, we are essentially living in a time of economic uncertainty and financial challenges.

Occasionally, I listen to friends, family members, and co-workers share their views on finances, and I sense that some of them think that financial education is for the poor and disadvantaged. Because they believe they are high-income earners who own their own homes, have registered retirement savings plans—albeit with limited funds in some cases, because most have no knowledge of the amount of investment required to maintain their current lifestyle after retirement—or a defined benefit pension, they believe they are living the best lifestyle for people in their social class. But regardless of how financially secure a person may feel, one's financial well-being can be quickly altered due to unexpected life circumstances. Some believe that should things take a turn for the worse in their financial standing, the government will pick up the pieces and care for them after retirement. What many of them don't realize is that the Canada Pension Plan and Social Security funds are running at a deficit. Plus, there's the matter of the maximum amount of retirement benefit that each person will receive. In this year, 2019, the maximum Canada Pension payout is $1,175.83, while the maximum Social Security payout is $2,861, if your payments start at age 65. And only retirees who made the maximum contributions each year are entitled to receiving the maximum payout. With 10,000 baby boomers retiring every day, these plans could become broke by the time all of them are retired.

Others believe it is only the less educated—people with low IQ and low literacy skills, or people with learning disabilities—who need financial education. In a paper on financial literacy, written by Leona English, she shared that some proponents of financial education, who developed programs, workshops, and websites to spread financial literacy, also believe that only the poor and under-educated need to become more financially literate. Some of them think that the poor and the less educated population are responsible for the dire economic conditions that some countries are now experiencing.

In fact, according to English, Mitt Romney, one of the candidates for the presidency of the United States in 2012, *"blamed the poor for the poor economy, saying that 47% of U.S. citizens are a drain on the government coffers and that they need to straighten up."*

The burning questions I have are: Since when are the poor responsible for education? Shouldn't the government and educational institutions be responsible for teaching financial literacy, the same way they are responsible for educating the population at large? How can adults be expected to demonstrate effective money management skills, to master personal finances for their unique circumstances, if they were not trained to do so? And don't you think financial education would equip even the less fortunate with the needed skills to manage their money effectively so that they are less dependent on the government? Is it possible that personal finance could improve the lifestyle of some of the people Mitt Romney referred to, and thus causing them to climb the social class ladder and be less dependent on the government? And is it possible that the government encourages some people to stay poor?

I'll let you be the judge of that.

A Short Conversation with a Tenant Applicant

Applicant: I am on government assistance, but I would like to rent-to-own a home so that I could eventually own something for myself and my kids.

Me: To participate in the rent-to-own program, you need to show proof of funds for the deposit.

Applicant: I do have some money for the deposit, from working on the side, but I'm not sure how to prove that electronically, because I don't have the money in the bank.

Me: Why don't you save in the bank; how would you get a mortgage?

Applicant: I can't save the money in the bank because the government will stop helping me if they see that I have some money. My kids are still young, and when I work some shifts, I have to pay a babysitter. But the government doesn't care about that; all they care about is that I'm making money. They don't realize that in order to make more money, I have to pay out some money, so I still need some help right now since the kids are still young and it's me alone.

There's also the matter of increasing the minimum wage to keep people holding on to menial jobs instead of encouraging them to improve themselves to be more employable. For example, in 2018, the government in the province of Ontario, in Canada, raved about raising the minimum wage, and about it being such a great move to help families. But I believe it was done to get people's votes. Many people bought into this idea, and cursed the subsequent government that decided to cancel promised increases. But what many people fail to realize is that the jobs that pay minimum wages should not be viewed as permanent jobs for family members.

And don't get me wrong; I know some people are happy with earning just minimum wage. But these jobs should be viewed as stepping stones on your way to improving yourself to increase your earning power. A higher minimum wage can cause people to become more complacent and remain poor. In fact, some of my students complained that their hours were slashed when the minimum wage increased, because employers didn't want to increase their costs. I suspect many non-student workers also experienced the same, because one month, two of my tenants complained that their income was much lower because their work hours were reduced drastically due to the minimum wage increase, so they had to seek additional employment elsewhere. My question therefore is, did increasing minimum wage really help Ontarians in those jobs, or did it reduce their earning power and force them to seek additional employment?

Students Have More Interest in Money

A research done by The British Psychology Society indicates that university students today are more motivated by money. The report said learning to become adept in a particular field appears to be secondary to millennials, compared to being able to get a job and make good money. This is unlike students from earlier generations, like the baby boomers, who valued education more. That is not to say the millennials do not value education, but the question is, what kind of education? They view traditional education as *"a transactional procedure or a means to an end."* And who can blame them? We live in a world that is so commercialized now. A lot of emphases is placed on appearance and owning material things these days, and students try to compete to be seen as equal. I believe if millennials could identify a way to achieve the material things and live the lifestyle they desire, many of them would not attend college, or perhaps they would drop out of college once they achieve their desired goals.

The typical response I get when I ask students who are struggling with math why they don't stay after school to get some extra help, is: *"I have to work Ms."* Whenever I try to lecture them that a better performance in school today will set them up for a better job later, and for greater success in the future, invariably, I get responses like: *"Ms., I have to buy my clothes and shoes, I have to pay for my cellphone, I have to pay for my car; I need money, Ms.,"* and the list goes on. I rarely get: *"I have to save for my tuition,"* or *"I have to help out my mom."* On a few occasions when I said, *"Oh, you're working because you're saving for your tuition,"* I get: *"Tuition? Oh no Ms., I will take a student loan for that."* So, my conclusion is that the desire to earn money is centered on acquiring material things. And websites like Google encourage students to feed into purchasing more and more material things. How?

Google has partnered with public schools across Canada, the US, and other countries around the world, so millions of students and teachers are using Google Drive, Google Docs, Google Slides, Google Classrooms, and other Google products daily. This gives Google access to students' and educators' personal information. Do you think Google does nothing with this data? It can track users' browsing history to target online advertising based on the search engine activity. Don't you find it strange when an advertising website randomly pops up on your screen when you're browsing, and that site may be one you visited before, or has items similar to ones that you have searched for prior? Do you think that was so random or a mere coincidence? Or is it possible that Google has been spying on you, and sharing your private data with vendors?

Having an interest in earning money is definitely not a bad thing, as that is what has driven many successful people, but as Johnathan Swift said: *"A wise person should have money in their head, but not in their heart."* So if young people are being driven increasingly by money, and they don't acquire the skills for good money sense and financial literacy, they will spend most of their pre- and post-retirement years trying to acquire more and more money. However, they will still wind up in bad debt, and have insufficient funds to last them through retirement.

Why Some Topics Engage Students More

The internet has provided a plethora of resources and information that students can access easily. This allows them to do their own research and identify the skills required for the careers they may want to pursue. In a society where a number of students struggle with math concepts, many tend to gravitate towards careers that require little or no math. Frequently, the essential math skills that are needed can be acquired by grade 10. For this reason, many students who are not pursuing math-related careers, have little or no interest in post grade 10 math. They see no relevance between math and their career choices. Some feel they're forced to cover additional math concepts for no apparent reason except that math is mandatory up to a particular grade level. In Canada, for example, high school math is compulsory from grade nine to grade 11, so every student must have a grade 11 math credit before they can receive their high school diploma.

While I have no issue with math being mandatory up to grade 11—in fact, I will go out on a limb here and say that I think it should be compulsory up to grade 12—I do not agree with a lot of the concepts that are in some of the grade 11 and 12 courses for the general population. For students pursuing careers as a math teacher, actuary, statistician, or financial analyst, for example, those concepts may be applicable. But for students who want to become a linguist, lawyer, journalist, or social worker, for instance, why do they need to learn about quadratic functions and trigonometry?

The labels given to some math courses should also be changed to remove the negative stigma attached to them, because some of the lower-level courses have more useful topics for everyday life than the higher-level ones. But because of the negative stigma attached to those lower-level courses, students don't want to be associated with them. If you heard grade 9 academic, grade 9 applied, and grade 9 essentials math, and you were pursuing law, for instance, which of these courses would you want to be associated with? How about grade 11 university, grade 11 college/university, grade 11 college, and grade 11 workplace? The grade 11 college and workplace courses have more financial application topics that would prove more useful to a lawyer than the university course. Yet, a budding lawyer would not want to be associated with those courses. They are perceived as courses for low performing students, and lawyers are viewed as high achievers.

Two of the most real-life application grade 11 and 12 courses that I've taught are called Math for Everyday Life. I totally agree that the concepts they cover are related to everyday life, so the name is very appropriate. However, because they are the destination courses for the students who did the grade 9 and 10 essential math courses, students still refer to them as the grade 11 and 12 essential math courses. For this reason, many parents do not want their children in an essential math course, whether they are college-bound or not. So, students look down on these courses and stigmatize them instead of gravitating towards them. They go for the university courses that sometimes have no relevance to their career choice…some of them repeating the courses up to 3 times before conceding.

And don't get me wrong; I'm not against repeating. Some people may have to try multiple times before they actually get it, which is quite alright. English was not my strong subject, and some of these sentences I had to rewrite up to three times before they really sounded like what I truly wanted to say...and no doubt my editor still changed some of them. But my point is, why do students keep repeating a course that has little relevance to where they are heading, because they don't want to be stigmatized? I have seen students who repeat and receive lower grades each time. That should say something, because repeating an activity should demonstrate improvement, not regression. Repetition is where the idea of practicing to perfection comes from. As the old adage says: *"Repetition is the mother of learning."* So, if students are repeating courses and performing more poorly, they are obviously not learning. However, if courses were designed more relevantly and named more appropriately, the stigma would be lost. And students would feel more comfortable pursuing what they prefer, and what makes more sense to them, instead of what boosts their self-esteem.

Let's look at some course titles:

- Actuarial Science Math
- Math for Everyday Life Application
- Math for Engineering and Computer Science
- Accounting and Financial Analyst Math
- Math for Natural Sciences

Which of these courses would you want to take for sure? I don't know about you, but Math for Everyday Life Applications would be the one I'd be most curious about. My point, however, is that these names would be more practical and relevant, and students would not run away from courses that are more beneficial to them. And they would not feel inadequate or inferior to the students who are pursuing the higher-level math courses that are applicable to their career path.

Why More Focus on Financial Applications Will Interest Students

My experience in the classroom, over the years, is that students will engage in learning when the concepts are practical and meaningful to them. They lose interest in learning when they cannot relate their learning to their lived experience, or they can't see where concepts will fit into where they are heading. Every student has an interest in money, whether it involves earning it, spending it, saving it, or sharing it. So they need to know how to handle money effectively—through budgeting, debt management, investing, and even giving/donating—at an early age. If more focus is placed on personal finance, and how students can develop healthy money habits to avoid mistakes that may lead to lifelong money woes, students will have more interest and will become more engaged in learning. They know money is an essential need. Without money, you cannot afford the basic physiological needs like food, water, and shelter.

Many students enter high school with no knowledge of the career they want to pursue. The field they choose to engage in will often depend on what they think will pay good money, what their friends decide to study, or what their parents convince them to pursue. Some of them go to college and university, and jump from program to program, because they don't like the courses that are offered, but they're not sure what they really want to do, or what really interests them. Some leave college with high student loan debt but can only get low-income jobs that don't provide enough to help them repay their loan. Others loved their programs but are still unable to find a good-paying job because their degrees are useless. Nowadays, if university programs are not in the STEM field, the remunerations are very low. Engineers and computer architects, for example, will be paid much more than a social worker.

Despite your interest and what you choose to become, if more financial application concepts are covered in school, that will give you the edge to identify strategies to increase or improve your earning power, even if the job you really love doesn't reward you enough financially. You could become an entrepreneur in the same field as a means to increase your earnings. But because the current education system trains you to become an employee, instead of teaching you to make money work for you, you and many others cannot see yourselves being anything but one. Many financially successful people are entrepreneurs because entrepreneurship is an integral part of financial education. So, despite the career you love and chose—and whether it results in high or low income—financial education is still something that you can benefit from to improve your earning potential and complement your lifestyle and well-being. Therefore, if it's taught in school, it will benefit the masses, and set up everyone for greater financial success in the future.

Why Math Should Emphasize More Real-Life Application Concepts

A Statistics Canada report, released in September 2018, shows that the average score for a 15-year-old student's performance in mathematics, from 2003 to 2015, as measured by the Programme for International Student Assessment (PISA), has dropped. And this decline is both at the OECD (Organisation for Economic Co-operation and Development) average, and for Canadian students. While the performance in reading is relatively the same for high school students in Canada, the trend in math performance is on the decline. When I researched what the situation was in the United States, the trend in the data was much the same, maybe even more concerning. A 2016

New York Times article, by Kate Zernike, says: "*The average performance of the nation's high school seniors dropped in math, from 2013 to 2015, but held steady in reading, according to results of a biennial test.*" The test results were released shortly before the article, and Zernike went on to say that "*the results from the National Assessment of Educational Progress also showed a drop in the percentage of students in private and public schools, who are considered prepared for college-level work in reading and math.*" When the study was done in 2013, 39% of students were estimated to be ready in math. However, two years later, there was a 2% drop in the number of students who were considered ready for college. Zernike says the performance at the lower grade was much the same too, because the results that were released the previous fall, also showed a similar decline in math.

The million-dollar question is: What is causing this decline in high school math performance? Is it pedagogy? Is it inadequate teacher training? Is it a reduced interest in learning math? Or is it a result of an outdated and irrelevant curriculum that is disconnected from the real world? In a previous section, I mentioned that students need to learn more about money and finances than they need to learn algebra. The results from the National Assessment illustrated that students were not doing well with algebra, but they were good with proportional reasoning. And this is not surprising, because proportional reasoning is a logical process that most students can relate to in their real lives, and make sense of, while algebra is very abstract and difficult to make connections to the real world. Consider the two scenarios below, involving money, with proportional reasoning and algebra:

> **Proportional Reasoning:** If 3 pounds of steak costs $45.60, and 4 pounds of chicken costs $12.20, how much will 8 pounds of steak and 10 pounds of chicken cost?

Algebra: If 3 pounds of steak and 4 pounds of chicken costs $57.80, while 4 pounds of steak and 3 pounds of chicken costs $69.95, how much will 8 pounds of steak and 10 pounds of chicken cost?

Stop reading now, and solve the problem using both scenarios.

Did you get: 8 pounds of steak costs $121.60
10 pounds of chicken costs $30.50

So the total cost is: $152.10 ($121.60 + $30.50)

How long did it take you to solve the problem using proportional reasoning? How long did it take you to solve the problem using algebra? You may have even given up trying to solve the problem using algebra.

What's the lesson here?

The end game for both scenarios was to determine the cost for 8 pounds of steak and 10 pounds of chicken. But the proportional reasoning was more logical and straight forward: Find the cost for 1 pound of steak by dividing $45.60 by 3, then find the cost of 1 pound of chicken by dividing $12.20 by 4. Once you know the unit price for steak and for chicken, you can find the cost for any number of pounds of each meat by multiplying the unit price by that number. Then you just need to add the two individual costs to get the total cost.

The algebraic method, however, requires that you use one variable to represent the cost for one pound of steak, and another variable to represent the cost for one pound of chicken. Then write down 2 different algebraic equations to represent the given information, and then solve the equations simultaneously. For those who couldn't solve the problem using algebra, I won't even waste any more of your time explaining how that is done. I will just stop here and let you decide if it doesn't make way more sense for math to emphasize more real-life application concepts that are logical and relatable, and that can be easily understood by the masses, than to emphasize more abstract concepts that are confusing and cause dissonance in learners.

Now that you understand that you don't need the abstract mathematical concepts to solve real-life problems involving money, and that you're actually using math daily, even though you may think differently, you are ready to read the next chapter, which discusses why financial literacy is important to manage your household expenses, and why everything that involves a monetary transaction, requires at least a moderate level of financial education to make smart decisions to build a strong financial foundation.

5
Financial Literacy Matters

"Fundamentally, the solution to economic insecurity is economic prosperity—an achievable goal. But for anyone who has grown up without financial security, there's a shadow that lies over even those who move towards independence: lack of financial literacy."

—Stacey Abrams

Managing Household Expenses

Ultimately, your household expenses depend on factors like your family size, and whether you own or rent your home. But expenses usually fall under six main categories:

1. Housing and Utilities
2. Food and Clothing
3. Health and Personal Care
4. Transportation
5. Insurance
6. Entertainment and Education
7. Savings and Investments

Some household expenses may add a miscellaneous category to put expenses like helping family members. For instance, many immigrants in Canada and the United States remit money to their families back home. It is essential that priorities are placed on your basic needs—the lowest on Maslow's Hierarchy of needs chart—before other needs and the needs of others come in to play.

Because commercialization is the front runner of our global economies, your priorities can be easily shifted if you're not disciplined, and you fail to budget appropriately. Gone are the days when you had to drive to the store to purchase everything. Purchasing items is now at your fingertips, and thanks to companies like Amazon, you can make a purchase in the night and have it on your porch before school is out the next day. A global economy that focuses on spending and acquiring material things, can have adverse effects on consumers who lack good money sense and don't spend wisely. You can't even open a website these days without seeing an advertisement distracting you to purchase something. There are even computer spyware that keeps track of sites that you visited before to buy or read reviews about an item.

These sites will pop up randomly, showing you items of interest to coerce you to purchase. And if that's not enough, they also have suggestion purchases, egging you on to buy more. Or you see the popular tag line: *People who purchased those items also purchased these*. So if you're not disciplined, you can potentially end up spending way more than you planned to. It happens to the best of us sometimes. I believe I'm a disciplined spender; but on occasions, I may go to purchase an outfit for a special occasion, and before I know it, I'm opening a box with two or three dresses that fit perfectly, and I don't have the willpower to return the unwanted ones.

Consequently, creating a budget to manage household expenses is very important. Every student should learn how to create a budget. A great exercise that everyone should do in school is to create a realistic household budget that mirrors their expected income, based on career choices and the lifestyle that they see themselves living in the future. For example, in the province of Ontario, in Canada, creating a budget is covered in the grade 12 college and everyday life math courses. The Ministry of Education obviously acknowledges the need for students to learn this. But if it's essential for those students, why isn't it essential for the academic and university math students as well? Is it that academic students don't need to do budgets, or is that the Ministry of Education expects them to figure that out on their own?

There is also the matter of fast food and Uber eats. Some parents aren't teaching children to cook anymore, and some children have no desire to learn how to cook. Why cook when you can do takeout delivery, or Uber eats? Plus, with Uber eats, households can now get food from restaurants, which don't do traditional delivery, delivered at their door. Depending on the choice of meals, takeout can cost a family much more than it costs to do home meals. And that can increase household expenses dramatically. Not to mention that it's healthier to cook at home—assuming you make healthy choices—than it is to eat out.

Here's an example of how delivery can easily rock up more expenses. I was at a house décor centre, in 2018, when a discussion about children loving Uber eats came up. During that discussion, the rep shared how annoyed she was with her niece, who thought the pizza they were having needed a special dipping sauce. And instead of foregoing the sauce that one time, her niece ordered Uber eats that cost more than twice what she would have paid for an entire bottle of dipping sauce.

Of course I'm not saying that delivery or takeout is all bad, because there are evenings when I'm exhausted and very glad they exist. But even when you do takeout, there are strategies that you can use to reduce the cost, such as picking up the food yourself. Some other strategies that you can employ to reduce household costs, are: using coupons; buying things on sale or clearance; having Netflix instead of using traditional cable for movies; buying a movie from pay-per-view or iTunes, which the family can watch instead of going to the movie theatre, where you have to pay for each person. Many other simple money-saving strategies can be utilized to reduce your household spending, leaving you with more money to save and invest for the future.

Buying a Home

When I was buying my first home, I thought I knew everything there was to know about buying a home: I checked out the listings in the area

I wanted to live; I did my research to compare various banks' interest rates; I got mortgage pre-approvals from different banks, to know what mortgage my income could afford; and I ascertained the down payment I would need, based on different mortgage ratios. I also calculated my monthly payment based on my payment frequency—monthly or bi-weekly—and how much I would be paying in interest based on my down payment and the amortization period. I even knew approximately how much to budget for closing costs, and that I could use my retirement funds contributions, without penalty, towards my down payment, thanks to my realtor. However, there were a few things that came up during the process that I believe would have prepared me better, if I knew about them prior to purchasing.

For starters: I wasn't familiar with the impact of a cashback mortgage, I never knew I could negotiate an interest rate, I wasn't familiar with a short mortgage term, I thought my mortgage payment would have been the same for the life of the mortgage, I didn't understand how mortgage insurance works, and I didn't know about mortgage prepayment or making extra payments. And I'm not saying that everyone was in my position when they were buying their first home, or that not knowing these things prevents you from getting a good rate, but I think knowing all these things ahead of time would have made my plans leading up to buying my first home a bit different. For instance, if I knew earlier that first time home buyers are able to use up to $25,000 of their registered retirement funds towards the down payment, with no tax withholding amounts, I would have contributed the funds I saved for my down payment, into a retirement savings plan. Making more contributions to my retirement funds would have given me a greater advantage. Why would it?

When I purchased my first home, I had only $2,600 in my retirement funds; most of my money was sitting in other accounts. Had I known that I could have used up to $25,000 of my retirement funds, with no withdrawal penalty, I would have contributed at least $25,000 to the plan. That amount would have reduced my income, thus giving me some tax refund, which I could have added to my savings as well. I would be forced to contribute back the $25,000 I borrowed from my retirement plan over 15 years, which is to my benefit because that meant I would be banking on myself. This is similar to when you take a loan from the bank. Over time, you have to pay back the loan with interest, but in this case, I would be borrowing the money from myself—interest-free—and I would have a specified time to pay myself back.

Understanding how prepayment works and how it impacts your mortgage interest over time is also advantageous. Most home buyers want to pay off their mortgage as fast as possible, and they believe having a higher mortgage obligation helps them to get there faster. Hence, they may opt for a 25-year amortization period instead of a 30-year period, because five more years seems much longer. But what they don't know is that having a lower obligation on paper works better in their favour. They can take a longer amortization period but make additional prepayments up to what the lending institution allows.

The beauty is that all prepayments reduce the mortgage principal instantly, but in months when there may be an unexpected significant expense, you can decide to use the prepayments to clear off that expense, with no effect to your mortgage obligations. Also, when you get a lump sum from tax returns, a cash gift from relatives, or perhaps some inheritance from the death of a loved one, you can make lump-sum prepayments to reduce your mortgage even more.

As these prepayments are made, the life of the mortgage keeps reducing. So, a 30-year mortgage can be quickly reduced to a 20-year mortgage, but your payment obligation is lower.

Having a lower mortgage payment also helps in situations when you may want a loan to start a business or invest in real estate. Your debt-service-ratio (DSR)—a ratio that lending institutions use to determine how creditworthy you are—is affected by your monthly obligations. Your DSR is a measurement of how much cash flow you have to service your debt. A simple formula to find your DSR is:

$$DSR = \frac{Monthly\ Cashflow}{Monthly\ Debt\ Service}$$

If your DSR is less than one, that means your cashflow is negative; you have more debt than you have money to cover. If your DSR is one, you have no cashflow, and you have just enough money to cover your debt. And if your DSR is greater than one, it means you have positive cashflow. A positive DSR doesn't necessarily mean you're in a good position, however, because a DSR that is close to 1 means you're just meeting your debt obligations.

When a lending institution is calculating your debt-service-ratio to determine what loan you may qualify for, the lower your monthly payment obligations, the lower your DSR, and the more advantage you have in getting a higher loan at a lower interest rate, because you will be considered a worthy creditor. Hence, it's better to keep your mortgage payments low on paper, but make double payments or lump-sum payments whenever you can, to reduce the mortgage quickly.

Saving for Emergency Expenses

Despite your plans and best efforts, life is very unpredictable. Unexpected expenses are things that everyone will experience at least five times in their lifetime. Frequently, these expenses pop up at a time that you may think is the worst timing, because you may be in the process of rebalancing your budget because of additional spending, or you may be saving for a special occasion. For instance, you may have just returned from a vacation, or the holiday season just ended, where you spent more on gifts and party preparations. To deal with these unforeseen expenses, it's a good idea to have an emergency fund. This is a pool of money that you set aside to help cover unanticipated expenses; for example, if your air conditioner dies in the middle of a sweltering summer, or your furnace dies in the heart of winter. It is like an insurance policy against life's unexpected expenses.

Many Canadians and Americans are two paychecks—tops—away from bankruptcy. They don't have enough saved up to carry their expanses for more than a month. The rule of thumb for emergency funds is that it should be able to cover your major expenses for four to six months. Not having an emergency fund could lead to a complete life-altering experience where your finances are concerned. Unlike Canada, which has a highly subsidized healthcare system for all its citizens and permanent residents, working-class citizens and permanent residents in the US are mostly responsible for their medical expenses. Before Barrack Obama introduced Obama Care, many Americans with no proper health insurance, who became sick unexpectedly, received medical bills that pushed them into financial woes that they may never recover from in their lifetime. And while having an emergency fund may not have made any difference for some people, it would have made a difference for many.

Having an emergency fund is not only about covering expenses; it can also give you peace of mind, which improves your lifestyle and well-being. If you don't already have an emergency fund, imagine how it would feel if tomorrow you woke up and your fairy godmother or godfather called to say: "I just opened an emergency fund for you, with $20,000, but the funds can only be used for unexpected expenses, because you'll need two signatures to withdraw the money." Did you already start daydreaming as if it were true? Did you feel a sense of calm come over you while you dreamed? That's because it gave you peace of mind—even though it wasn't real. In your little daydream, you felt secure, and you felt free from the pressures of the unknown.

Maybe you're at that stage in your relationship where you want out. Or you want to start that little business you keep dreaming about every night. Perhaps you just want to complete that master's degree that you couldn't finish because of a lack of funds. The point is, having an emergency fund can undoubtedly give you the freedom to leave that relationship, start that new business, or complete that master's. The key to saving towards an emergency fund is that the account should be separate from the account you use regularly. The savings should be done on a regular basis, and it's even better if it's automatic. For example, setting up an automatic savings plan that sends an amount to your emergency funds account, each time you get paid, will prevent you from spending frivolously. As the saying goes, *out of sight, out of mind*. If you don't see the money, you won't remember it is there, and you certainly won't spend it on things you don't need. So, your unexpected expenses insurance policy will be safe.

Saving for Your Children's Education

It is great that students whose parents are unable to pay for their education still have an opportunity to attend college or university because of student loans. But this is a debt that hangs around students' necks the moment they enter college. And this debt increases each year until they complete their program of study. In 2018, reports in Canada and the United States identified student loan debt as the second highest consumer debt category, mortgage debt being the highest. Collectively, Canadian students owe more than $28 billion in student loans to all levels of government, while US students owe $1.5 trillion. Robert Kiyosaki, in his book, *Fake,* said that student loan debt is the number one asset for the American government. It's mind-boggling to think that the US government's best asset is predicated on capitalizing on its residents' inability to pay cash for education.

A 2017 article, by Kristen Kuchar, a US writer and editor, states that 19% of borrowers in the US owe more than $50,000 in student loan debt upon graduation. But there are a few people who owe more than $1 million in student loans. Can you imagine having a loan for more than a million dollars, when it would take you 10 years to earn $1 million if your gross income was $100,000 per year? And do keep in mind that your net income would be less than three-quarters of your gross, which is less than $75,000. How many years do you think it would take you to repay this loan? When I calculated the monthly payment for a 1-million dollar loan at 5% annual interest for 100 years, the monthly payment is $4195.23. This is why some parents are still repaying student loans after their own children complete university.

One day, I was listening to the Wall Street Journal podcast, *Your Money Briefing*, and Cezary Podkul was explaining why some bonds tied to student loans won't mature until the 2070s and later. As an example, he talked about a nurse who had student loans for about $250,000, whose payments were reduced considerably to a more affordable one because she couldn't afford to repay within the specified time. As a result, the bonds tied to her loan could be at risk of downgrading, because the bond maturity date would be before her loan is paid off. To avoid the bonds from downgrading, the maturity date was pushed well beyond her life expectancy—more than 110 years. Since the government guaranteed these bonds, it means taxpayers would shoulder the rest of her student loan if she doesn't repay in full before she dies. But what is the probability that she will live to 110 years?

Can this be avoided?

Yes, it can! Early and proper planning for college expenses can avoid the high student loan debt that many people have after college. There are various strategies that can be applied to prevent this. For instance, if you buy insurance that has a cash value benefit for your children, from when they are babies, because of compounding interest, the cash benefit will grow to a considerable amount that can be used for college expenses. Another option is to open a registered education plan. This plan may be an individual or a family plan. The advantage of having a registered education plan is that in America, for example, you can lock in today's tuition cost for your children, even though they would be attending college later. And, in other countries like Canada, the government will match your contributions by a percentage up to a certain limit.

The US has education savings plans like the *529 College Plan,* the *Roth IRA,* and the *Prepaid College Tuition Plan.* Canada has the *Registered Education Savings Plan (RESP).* While I'm not a big fan of any of these plans, especially since the interest earned on them is usually low, I believe any education saving plan is better than no education savings plan. In Canada, for instance, the government will contribute 20% on contributions up to $2500 per year—a maximum of $500 per year by government—to a maximum contribution of $7200, by the time the child is 18. You would think the government would cap at $9000 instead, which gives 18 years of contribution.

Eighteen is the common age at which students enter their first year of college or university, and I believe that if the government would give 18 years of contribution, then that would encourage parents to start saving early—from the year the child is born—to capture all the benefits. Contributions for only fourteen years encourage some parents to procrastinate, thinking they have enough time to still capture the 14 years maximum grant if they start later. But despite best intentions, some parents just never get back around to doing it, or monthly expenses become more of a priority.

Some people invest in real estate as a strategy to not only pay for their child's education, but to also have a home waiting for him at the end of college. How does real estate help to pay for your children's education?

If an investment home is purchased when the child is five years old, for instance, when the child is 18, the home will have 13 years of equity from the mortgage paydown—paid by the tenants—and the home appreciation. The parents can refinance the home to get back their down payment and more, and then use this amount to pay for tuition and other college expenses. Upon completion of university, the child will have no student loan, and the home is still there for him.

Personally, I used a combination of RESPs and real estate to save for my sons' college expenses. Although I don't like RESPs, my main reason for using them was to capture the government grant, and not put all my eggs in one basket, so to speak. If I had been knowledgeable about the use of insurance, from when they were younger, I would have used that too. However, despite the strategies you decide to use, the key is to start planning early. Whether you will be contributing to an education fund, using insurance, or real estate, the sooner you start investing, the more time and potential your money will have to grow to a large sum to cover increasing college tuition.

Student Loan Interest Rate

CNBC reported that the US interest rate on new undergraduate loans, for the 2018–2019 academic year, is 5.05%, which is a 0.6% hike from the previous year. But that rate is not the same across the board. Graduate students pay 6.6% interest rate, while professional graduate students and parents of undergrad students have to pay 7.6%. On December 5, 2018, the Government of Canada updated student loan rates to the prime lending rate + 2.5% for the variable rate, and prime rate + 5% for the fixed rate. This translates to 6.45% and 8.95%, respectively, on the day that I wrote this paragraph.

Let's look at a loan calculation using the US undergrad rate of 5.05%, since it's the lowest rate; then the Canadian fixed rate of 8.95%, since it is the highest. I will use a conservative loan amount of $25,000, and assume you will pay back the loan in 10 years. You don't have to know how to calculate this; there are many online loan calculators or loan apps on your smartphones to do the calculations for you.

Example 1
 Loan Amount = $25,000
 Interest Rate = 5.05%
 Term = 10 years
 Monthly Payment: $265.78
 Total Interest Paid = 6893.02

Example 2
 Loan Amount = $25,000
 Interest Rate = 8.95%
 Term = 10 years
 Monthly Payment: $316.01
 Total Interest Paid = $12921.60

How much did you pay or are expecting to pay for your own or your children's tuition? My older son is pursuing film production at York University in Toronto. Currently, I am paying close to $10,000 per year for tuition alone. If I include his boarding, food, transportation, books and supplies, and other school-related expenses, it's costing me more than $25,000 per year for him. Imagine the loan he would be saddled with upon completion, and the interest he would have to pay. The combination of a registered education savings plan and investing in real estate definitely made a huge difference for me.

Something I stumbled on when I was researching for this section, is that in Canada, student loans can be forgiven for nurses and family doctors who started their employment after July 1, 2011, in underserved rural or remote communities. If you think you may be eligible, all information can be obtained from the Canadian government website. And if you're currently pursuing studies in one of these careers, you could consider moving to work in one of these qualified areas afterward. You would not only be helping yourself, but also helping people to get medical care in those regions where there's a shortage of care.

I know the reality for some parents is that household expenses limit their ability to save. One suggestion is to participate in something like the *Gift of College Program* in the US. Essentially, this program allows family members and friends to contribute monetary gifts to your children's education savings plan, for those gifting occasions. So, instead of buying toys and clothes for birthdays and Christmas gifts, parents can ask loved ones to gift money toward the children's education. I couldn't find any official program like this in Canada, but it's a great idea that can be emulated in any country. Over a period of 18 years, monetary gifts can be invested, and grow to cover or reduce your children's university costs so that they have less or no debt upon graduation. There is also a bonus if the monetary gifts are deposited in a registered education savings plan, in countries like Canada where the government matches the contributions by 20%.

Investing in Yourself

There are different methods that you can use to invest in yourself, but I will focus on two simple strategies here:

1. Pay yourself first, before you pay others.
2. Bank on yourself or bank on your family members.

Pay yourself first is a concept I learned when I read *The Wealthy Barber,* by David Chilton, and it really stuck with me. If I knew about this strategy before I got my first paycheck, I believe I would have been way more financially successful today. It is a common practice for everyone to pay their bills and buy things first, upon receiving their paychecks. For some, most months, there is no money left over to save by the time they take stock of their spending. But what if everyone was paying themselves 10% of their income first? Isn't that what the government forces most employees to do? Unless you have a business or you're a certain type of worker, the government doesn't allow you to get your paycheck, pay your bills, buy whatever you want, and then pay your income tax. The government takes your income tax, social security or pension, and unemployment insurance from your paycheck first, and then leaves the balance for you. So why not pay yourself before you pay the insurance and utility companies, the landlord or the mortgagor, and before you start spending your money?

Some of you may be asking, how can I pay myself 10% when there's not enough to go around? Try to answer this question: Has the government ever asked you if you have enough money to go around, before taking your income tax? So why do you need to ask yourself that? Pay yourself first, and make do with what's leftover. Maybe it means you drink water instead of buying pop, you cook more and eat out less, you make coffee at home instead of going to Tim Hortons or Starbucks, you go to the movies every other month instead of once a month, or you have to drop the expensive smoking habit. And if you're rolling your eyes and saying you do none of those, my point is, when you have less to spend, you'll find a way to make it work. Some people would still have nothing to save even if they weren't paying the income tax, so I'm sure you get my drift. And if you really can't start at 10%, try to start at even 2%, and gradually increase it over time. Humans are creatures of habit, so if you get in the habit of saving a little money regularly, saving will eventually become a way of life.

What is "Bank on Yourself"?

If you read Pamela Yellen's book, *Bank on Yourself*, you will understand more of what I'm going to explain. However, Pamela focused on insurance, but I won't. I am going to share how I use that same concept with my personal savings and my children's savings.

Above, I said you should first pay yourself 10% before you pay anyone else, and I subscribe to that. I suspect I pay myself more than 10% every month; that's because bills such as property taxes aren't due every month, but I save in advance to pay my taxes. So, I have automatic savings that go from my account to different accounts, which I call money buckets: I have a savings bucket for regular savings; a vacation bucket, where I save for vacations; I have a tax bucket, where I save for my property tax; and I have a maintenance bucket, where I put money for unexpected expenses.

For the tax bucket, for example, I divide my taxes by 12, and each month, that amount automatically goes from my checking account to the tax bucket. Now, suppose I have an unexpected expense, like the time my car's power steering pump failed, and when I went to pick it up, my service guy gave me a bill for $1700 plus change. If there are not enough funds in the maintenance bucket to cover the service and repair cost, I will borrow money from the tax bucket to help pay for it, but I pay back the tax bucket at a higher interest rate than on my line of credit. Why? Well, if I had no money buckets, and I had to borrow the money from my line of credit, I would have to pay the bank interest. If I have no qualms paying the bank interest, why not pay myself even more? After all, I did borrow the money, albeit from myself.

I call this situation "banking on yourself"…you become your own bank… paying yourself the interest you would have normally given to the bank.

Another Bank on Yourself Example

There have been occasions when a few of my properties need repairs simultaneously. In order to not deplete my business account, I may decide that a business loan to help cover expenses is necessary. But do I run to the bank for that loan? Of course not! I run to my money buckets. But what if my buckets fall short? I run to my sons' savings. I negotiate an interest rate with them, draft a business agreement, and the business repays them over time. Why give the bank more interest when you can give your own children or other family members the interest instead? I call this "banking on your family members."

All these are examples of strategies to invest in yourself—whether it is directly or indirectly. Vacations are very important for me. They give me a sense of renewal—getting away from the robotic life and just unwinding. As such, I consider investing in my vacation bucket as investing in myself. You may have something different that is important to you. Invest in that bucket. When I help my children to increase their savings and learn financial literacy skills in the process, I consider that to be an investment in myself, because that will help them to become financially independent at an earlier age, thus freeing me from their financial responsibilities sooner than later.

Investing for Your Retirement

Recent statistics show that more than one-third of North Americans do not have any savings or investments. At the end of the first quarter of 2019, the population of Canada and America surpassed 366 million. If the statistics are correct, this would mean that more than 120 million North Americans do not have a retirement savings plan. In fact, many of those who have savings plans will run out of money quickly after retirement, because the amount saved is not enough to last more than five years. In Canada, for instance, the average savings in a registered retirement savings plan is less than $60,000. This amount is less than twice the average yearly income in Canada, so how far can $60,000 go, especially since any money withdrawn will be taxed?

As of October 2018, on average, Canadians owe $1.78 for every $1 in disposable income they earn in a year. This is an 8% increase over a 4-year period. If this trend continues, when interest rates start to increase again, many people may find themselves in deeper financial problems. This could mean that some consumers will spend the rest of their working lives, and perhaps time into retirement, repaying debt. Moreover, some may never be able to save for their retirement, which means they would be entirely dependent on government and/or family members for support to live throughout their retirement years. But how much help will governments be able to provide over the next two decades when they're increasingly accumulating more debt. James Rickards, in his book, *The New Case for Gold*, says the US has 4.45 trillion dollars in liabilities. According to Trading Economics, Canada's debt increased from 671.3 billion dollars, in 2018, to 685.5 billion, in 2019, although I heard other news reported that it's actually more than 700 billion dollars.

There are more than 75 million baby boomers in North America—people born between 1946 and 1964—and every day, about 10,000 of them hit the retirement age. If that number of boomers retire daily, this means, every year, North American governments will be paying an additional 3.5 million people social security and Canada Pension. Eventually, the government coffers will be drained, since fewer and fewer people are paying social security and Canada Pension as the era of artificial intelligence evolves. Not to mention the fact that more people are living longer with advanced medicine. Therefore, the billion-dollar question is: How much longer will North American governments be able to provide for people with no retirement plan?

Everyone should be saving for their retirement; you should not be depending on the government to take care of you when you retire. But can you blame some people for not saving for the future; are they at fault? Did school teach them the importance of saving for retirement, and how to save for it? Do a mental reflection, and see if you can remember the first time you heard about a registered retirement savings plan (RRSP), if you're in Canada, or an individual retirement account (IRA), if you're in the United States. Do you fully understand how they work? Take the RRSP in Canada, for example; I didn't know that banks can withhold up to 30% of your RRSP contribution—if you withdraw—until my husband, Richard, was laid off when I was supposed to be on maternity leave, and I was researching to weigh my options where finances were concerned.

On top of this, for a while I thought I could only invest my RRSP in mutual funds. And since I'm not a big fan of mutual funds, I opted for saving in GICs and later in tax-free savings accounts. To earn more return on investment, I then used my savings to invest in real estate. Ironically, my real estate investment journey was born from a lack of proper financial education, so perhaps in some sense, I should be thanking the government for not teaching me financial literacy skills. I knew from when I was a young adult that there are far more returns on investing in real estate than in mutual funds. I saw how my home in Jamaica had appreciated in value after immigrating to Canada. I also didn't like that my money was tied up in an RRSP, and I had little control over how I could invest it—at least that's what I thought before I acquired more financial education.

I started recontributing in RRSPs a few years ago when I was tapped out and denied mortgages to purchase more homes. At the time, my bank said I shouldn't own more than five investment properties. And it didn't matter that I had the down payment to purchase more homes. In my quest for more knowledge, to determine how I could own more properties, I learned about private mortgages involving other peoples' RRSPs, and self-directed RRSP investments.

What is a self-directed RRSP?

This is where you transfer your RRSP to a trust company like Olympia Trust in Canada, and from there you can invest in companies like Pulis Investment Group, which invests in real estate and storage facilities, and GreyBrook Capital that does land development projects. These are government regulated companies, and they allow you to invest in passive real estate ventures. The return on these investments is much higher than on the traditional mutual funds that are loaded with fees, especially since you pay fees even when the funds aren't performing. Hence, these provide opportunities to grow my retirement funds much faster. So, I have a renewed view of RRSPs because not only do I get the tax returns from the contributions I make, I can also invest the funds in non-traditional mutual funds that give higher returns, and there's no fluctuation due to the stock market performance.

Whether you choose to invest in an RRSP, an IRA, real estate, or other types of retirement investments, any retirement investment is better than no investment at all. Furthermore, some employers match your retirement contributions, so you should capitalize on benefits like these if your employer offers them—even though these are usually group retirement funds, and you have no say in how your money is invested. And the earlier you start investing for retirement, the better the returns. Interest rates may be low now, but they won't remain low forever, and you want to have something baking in the oven when rates start to go up. Join me in the next chapter to learn why young people need financial education to begin conducting their financial affairs effectively from an early age, and why the sooner they start doing this, the more financially successful they will be before and after retirement.

6
Teaching Young People Financial Literacy

"Business leaders regularly complain that young people don't leave school with the right skills. Encouraging young people to be entrepreneurs makes the connection between school and the world of work, teaching them about practical thinking, teamwork, communication, and financial literacy."

—Steph McGovern

Creating a Budget

In order to secure a healthy financial future, young people must be able to make sound financial decisions. Many folks find themselves in financial crises because they fail to plan and keep track of their spending and expenses. Some marriages fail because money became a contentious issue that led to arguments and irreconcilable differences. In fact, financial issues are one of the top 5 reasons why marriages fail, and many divorces could have been avoided if couples had just taken the time to sit down together to create a financial agenda or a budget, and discuss their financial health on a regular basis.

What is a budget? A budget is a great way to plan and keep track of your finances. It is like a financial road map—a GPS—that shows the income, expenses, and savings for an individual or a family over a period of time. If used ritually, a budget can save you hundreds, and maybe even thousands, of dollars over time. This is because it forces you to be more disciplined with your money, since it makes you become more mindful of your spending habits. It makes you aware of how much money you have coming in and how much is going out, and you can also see where most of your money is going, and make adjustment in your monthly spending if necessary.

Even though creating a budget may sound complex and difficult, you don't need a degree to create one. In fact, Henry Paulson said: *"There's a great lack of financial literacy and understanding in this nation, even among college-educated people."* So, no doubt there are college-educated people who can't create a budget. You just need to have knowledge regarding the amount of income that you, or you and your spouse, will receive over a specific time period, and how you plan to use that income within that same time. The more simple your budget is, the easier it is for you to follow, and the more likely you will feel inclined to visit it regularly. Many user-friendly budget templates can be found online that are more or less the same. Although there may be subtle differences in the templates, the main categories below, for instance, will be on all of them.

- Housing
- Utilities
- Food
- Clothing
- Transportation
- Savings
- Entertainment

There are even budget apps on your smartphones, which you can use to keep track of your income, savings, and expenses. And once you have a working budget in place, it's just a matter of staying on top of things. If young people learn from an early age the importance of having a budget, and learn how to create one and use it to keep abreast of their finances, by the time they enter into relationships or marriages, they will have the hang of how to be good financial planners. My mom once said: *"When we learn how to effectively manage less, God knows we are better able to manage more, so he'll give us more."* I don't know if that's an old adage or whether she made it up on the spot, but there is a lot of wisdom in those words, and I truly believed them.

Since communication about finances is a sore point in many relationships, couples who make budgeting an integral part of their planning together will provide a framework to avoid conflicts relating to money. Besides, it can help couples to set savings or investment goals, whether short, medium, or long-term goals, to improve their lifestyle and well-being overtime. This could create a stronger bond between them, and hence lead to more successful marriages and relationships, not to mention a reduction in the number of divorces.

Managing Your Credit Cards

I believe that the credit card is one of the best inventions for consumers. Unfortunately, many consumers fall prey to them because they don't know how to use them wisely. Here are some of the reasons they are suitable for consumers:

1. They can be used to extend your spending ability.
2. They can be used to help manage your finances.
3. They give access to spending money that is interest free for the grace period.
4. They give reward points to redeem for purchases, bill payment, gift cards, airline tickets, and more.
5. They offer balance transfer at 0% or a much reduced interest rate, which you can use to pay off balances at higher interest rates, and consolidate debts into one monthly payment.
6. Some credit cards offer introductory balance transfers of 0% for up to 18 months.
7. Some credit cards offer 0% introductory rates on purchases for up to 21 months.
8. Some offer insurance for travel, rental cars, and trip cancellation and interruptions.
9. Most credit cards have no annual fee.
10. You're not on the hook for fraudulent transactions.

While I cannot say this is true for all credit card companies, my experience with a few of my credit card companies is that they take responsibility to dispute purchase dissatisfaction so that I get my refund, and on one occasion when I purchased airline tickets, and the company went out of business before I travelled, I was refunded the transaction even though the purchase was made nine months prior.

Before you choose a credit card, you should first consider how you plan to use it, to see which type of credit card would best suit your situation. Here are some of the questions you should ask yourself:

1. Does the card have an annual fee?
2. If there is an annual fee, does it cover travel and rental insurance, etc.?
3. Does the card have a reward program? (Most, if not all, offer reward points these days.)
4. How does that card's reward program work?
5. Will I be carrying a balance? (You shouldn't be carrying a balance, but if you think you will, look for a card with a lower interest rate and a longer grace period.)
6. Can I choose my bill payment date? (Having all bills due around the same time each month is a bad idea. Where possible, pace your bills so that they are due in different pay cycles.)

A great way to manage credit card payment is to set up automatic bill payment from your bank account. You have the option to set up automatic payment for the full amount or for the minimum payment. My son used to forget to pay his credit card bill sometimes, which would have messed up his credit if Richard didn't notice in time. To prevent this from happening, Richard set up automatic payment for the minimum amount. That way, even if my son forgets, at least the minimum is paid, and his credit stays intact.

I use credit cards to purchase almost everything, to optimize my reward points. Sometimes when I share this with people, they look at me puzzled. At first, I couldn't understand why I would get the puzzled look, until my card got compromised and I was talking to a representative at the bank. When I shared that I needed my replacement card as soon as possible because I use it to purchase pretty much everything, she immediately asked why I would do that, when the credit card interest is so high. I almost fell off my seat because I couldn't believe someone working in the credit card department would say something like that.

I slowly responded that I've never paid interest on any of my credit cards before; I've only gained interest from credit cards. And I was being truthful because that was before we started our real estate investments, where I use balance transfer on credit cards to save on business-related interest. Suffice to say, the rep got a free lesson on credit card usage before the call was over. It didn't occur to her that some people pay their credit card bill in full every month. She thought everyone carried a balance each month, hence the name, *credit card*. This is a prime example that things like these should be taught in school. There I was, talking to someone working in the financial product department, but she didn't fully understand how it works.

I also believe having a single credit card is not the wisest option for you, since if you're like me, who puts almost all purchases on the card, everything will be due at the same time. If you have only one card, you're unable to stagger your usage and payments. Here's what I do: I make an effort to know the billing period for the two main credit cards I use for consumer purchases, and I usually try to use the card with the later cut-off period at all times. This gives me the longest time to pay, especially for big-ticket items.

Let me use a personal example to explain a bit more here. One year, my microwave died, in January. The replacement and installation cost was almost $1000. January is my poorest month because the Christmas expenses are usually due. Having no microwave didn't just mean lots of inconveniences; since it's an over-the-range one, it meant that I had no fan to vent the food smell while cooking. But since it's a big-ticket item, I really wanted the purchase on the card I use for travel rewards, but I also wanted the longest time to pay for it. However, there was still one more week before the billing period for that card's cut-off date, and if I made the purchase then, that bill would be due February 15th. So, what did I do? I waited for the billing cycle to end, and purchased the microwave the day after. Hence, I had until March 15th to pay the bill, instead of February 15th. Therefore, Richard and I had four additional paychecks in total before we had to pay for the microwave. So, it was very easy for us to pay the bill in full without incurring any additional cost.

Building and Protecting Your Credit

Your credit report gives a summary of your payment history, your credit cards, and your borrowing activities over time. Lenders use it to determine how responsible you are with managing your financial obligations. Your report also has a credit score, which is a number that credit bureaus, like Equifax, TransUnion, and Experian, assign to you based on the information on your credit report. In Canada, the score ranges from 300 to 900 points. In the US, the score range is 300 to 850 points. Both Canada and the US consider a credit score of 680 to be average. But obviously, the higher the number, the greater your chance is of getting credit at lower interest rates.

I must admit that credit score is one of the topics relating to finances that I took the longest to understand. And this was mostly because I was listening to people who I believed knew what they were talking about, instead of researching it myself. The notion of having a good credit history or excellent credit scores is not something that was used in Jamaica when I was living there. In fact, I can't even remember the criteria by which I was judged to be eligible for a credit card in Jamaica, but I do remember having three different credit cards before I migrated. The first time I heard the term 'credit score' was when I went to the US as an undergrad student, on a work and travel program.

I remember going to Circuit City to purchase a cell phone, and the salesperson said that he needed my social security number because he had to check my credit. That was very foreign for me at the time, but I wanted the phone, and he insisted he needed it. My loved ones had shared that I should protect my social security number from fraudulent activities, so I decided he wasn't going to get it until it made sense for me to give it to him. When he realized I wasn't forthcoming, he painfully tried to explain why he needed it, and failed miserably. His supervisor eventually came but did a botched-up job too, and perhaps I felt sorry for them both, or I got tired, but I eventually gave in. The resounding feedback I got was that I had no credit, so they couldn't sell me the phone. It wasn't until after I asked why I needed credit to purchase a phone, when I had money, that the poor guy realized I wasn't living in the US, and therefore I didn't need a cellphone plan. He was so programmed to do a credit check that he automatically assumed he had to do one for me.

When I tried to purchase my first car in Canada, I had a similar experience but with a better outcome. Honda said I couldn't get financing or leasing because I had no credit. I told the salesperson that it made no sense that

I couldn't get financing, when I had enough money in the Royal Bank of Canada (RBC) to purchase the car with cash. Of course, I had no intention of buying the car cash, but the point is that I could have if I wanted to. The salesperson—God bless his soul—was determined to get us that car, and so he got RBC to agree to a Royal Buy Back for me, which was essentially a lease at twice Honda's interest rate at the time. On top of that, he explained that once I made the payments on time each month, my credit would start building, and I could refinance later, at a better interest rate. Sweet fellow! That was my first crash course on credit history and credit scores.

What he didn't share, however, was what would give me higher or lower scores, and this is the part that took me longer to understand, because I was listening to too many different theories. Luckily, you don't have to listen to false theories. While I cannot give you a specific formula—only people at the bureaus may have one—here, I will explain how your credit score is calculated. There are five key factors that credit bureaus use when calculating and determining your credit score:

1. Payment History: Are your payments made late or on time? (This counts for 35%.)
2. Total Amount Owed: Ideally, you want to keep your usage below 30%. (This counts for 30%.)
3. Length of Credit History: How long did you have your loan or credit cards? (This counts for 15%.)
4. New Credit Application: How many new loans or credit cards did you receive within the last two years? (This counts for 10%.)
5. Types of Credit Used: Are they credit cards, mortgages, LOC, a car loan, etc.? (This counts for 10%.)

Number two is where I was misled the most. I was mostly told that having too much credit was not good, so I was encouraged to have only 1 or 2 credit cards, and that I should ignore the limit increases. What I wasn't told was that if I have a credit card with a $10,000 limit, for example, and I use it to make $6500 in purchases every month, even if I pay my bill in full each month, the bureaus still view my usage as 65%. But if I had a limit of $30,000, and I use $6500 every month, my usage would be only 22%. In both scenarios, my usage is the same, but which one do you think would negatively impact my score?

Knowing how your credit score is calculated is important, because having a higher score gives you more negotiating power to get lower interest rates when you're applying for a loan or a mortgage. And what I have observed over the years is that I get a higher credit limit if I apply for a credit card when my score is excellent. I also get regular credit card promotions and credit limit increase offers, because financial institutions view me as a worthy creditor, even though I have about 10 different credit cards. Of course some cards are joint accounts with Richard. The one drawback with having 10 cards, however, is that you have to keep all 10 active so your credit score is not affected due to inactivity. To avoid this problem, I use some cards for monthly or yearly subscriptions only, and they are paid automatically, so I don't have to think about them until a replacement card comes in the mail when a card is about to expire.

Why 10 credit cards you may be asking? Before I was eligible to get business credit cards, I had to use my personal cards for business purchases. Sometimes purchases were high if I was refurbishing a property, for instance. Even though the bills were paid in full each month, those large purchases would negatively affect my personal credit score when my usage was close to, or greater than

30%. To prevent the negative impact, I applied for more credit to raise my overall credit limit to reduce my percentage usage. And even though I no longer have to use my personal cards for business purposes, I still keep all of them since the percentage usage for my own purchases is even more reduced with the higher credit limit, thus helping me to maintain a higher score than I would have if my overall limit was lower.

Lines of Credit Vs Credit Cards

Having a line of credit (LOC) and at least one credit card is definitely something that I recommend for you, because I believe everyone can run into a scenario where there's suddenly an unexpected need to access some cash quickly. Although the interest rate on LOCs is usually much lower than that on credit cards, it's way easier to access money from a credit card than it is to access funds from a LOC. Hence, depending on the situation, it may be wiser to use the credit card, and then pay the credit card bill from the line of credit account, if you have insufficient funds to pay the balance in full.

Let me use an example to explain more. In 2010, when I was house shopping, I saw my ideal home and wanted to put in an offer. My realtor thought the listed price was low for the calibre of home, and she shared that she suspected the selling realtor was trying to attract a bidding scenario. For this reason, she said it would be a good idea to increase my deposit to show the sellers that I was very motivated and had what it takes.

Although I had the funds I needed, it wasn't easily accessible. I needed to transfer some funds from one bank to another, and at that time, the funds could have taken up to 2 days to become available. I didn't want to miss the opportunity to put in an offer, however, so I got creative. I do most of my daily banking with The Royal Bank of Canada (RBC), so that was where I had my deposit for the offer on the home. But at the time, most of my savings were at ING Direct Bank—now called Tangerine—and my LOCs are at the Scotia Bank. So, to get the bank draft for the full deposit, I told my realtor that I would take a cash advance on my RBC credit card—at a whopping 13.99% interest rate—to make up the amount.

Once I got home, however—thanks to online banking—I paid the RBC credit card bill from my Scotia LOC (interest rate was 3%), and then I transferred funds from ING to my Scotia LOC. In the end, the amount of interest I paid was very negligible—one day for the credit card, and one day for the LOC, because all the funds got to their destination a day later. That was a very small price to pay to improve my probability of being chosen as the purchaser for the home I really wanted.

The takeaway here is that having credit at even a very high interest rate is better than no credit at all. Plus, that high-interest credit can become very useful at times, and depending on the circumstances, it doesn't necessarily mean your interest payment will be high. I didn't end up getting that home—in fact, no one did, since the seller later took the home off the market—but my fighting chance would have been nil if I didn't have the option to juggle my funds. Financial literacy, plus discipline, can make a huge difference in the choices you make, and your ability to seize the opportunities you're given.

Although credit cards have their place, it is always wise to remember that if you can't afford to pay your balance by the due date, the cost for your purchases can become way more expensive than what you actually paid, due to high-interest charges. So, if you're currently carrying a balance on your credit card, I suggest you transfer that balance to your LOC to reduce the amount of interest you pay. And try to pay off that balance before you make any more unnecessary purchases.

Here's a quick comparison between credit cards and lines of credit:

- Many credit cards offer low-interest promotional rates. Some come with a 0% introductory interest rate on initial purchases and balance transfers, and may even have a 0% balance transfer fee if the transfer is done within the first few months of getting the card. I have never seen a line of credit with a 0% introductory rate, but I do get low-interest promotional rates from time to time.

- Both have a minimum payment. For lines of credit, the minimum payment is the interest, while for credit cards, the minimum payment is usually a percentage, such as 1% of your outstanding balance.

- Credit cards give you a grace period, usually of at least 21 days—plus, don't forget, you also get that no-interest period between your purchase date and the bill cut-off date—but there is no grace period with lines of credit.

- If you pay your credit card balance in full, your interest charges will be 0. If you're only making the minimum monthly payment on your credit card, however, the grace period doesn't apply. Interest is charged for each day your balance is not paid up in full. Even new purchases attract daily interest. So, in this scenario, your credit card and LOC are treated similarly, except the LOC would be better since it attracts simple interest, while credit cards attract compound interest.

- Credit cards tend to offer reward programs, while lines of credit don't. But some credit cards with reward programs may have an annual fee, while lines of credit never have annual fees.

- Most credit cards now charge fees for cash advances—some never used to charge a fee—while lines of credit have no cash advance fees.

- Credit cards are usually unsecured and have high-interest rates. Lines of credit can be unsecured too, but many people have them secured, and a home is used as the collateral. For this reason, lines of credit attract lower interest rates. But even the unsecured ones have a lower rate than credit cards do.

There are many different types of credit cards—some have annual fees; some have lower interest rates, ranging from 10% to 15%; some have higher interest rates, ranging from 15% to 29%; and some have a reward program. So, when you're applying for a card, it's wise to shop around to determine the card that best suits your situation. A line of credit is usually more straight forward because there are only two options: secured or unsecured. A secured LOC is usually a home equity one, called a HELOC, and this one is more preferred because it is secured against your home. For this reason, the interest rate is much lower—it could be as low as the prime interest rate, like I have on one of mine.

Using Insurance to Increase Wealth

Many people view insurance as just peace of mind or a safety net in the event of unexpected life events, such as a motor vehicle accident, damage to a home, or the death of a loved one. But there is more to insurance than how most people consider it traditionally. Insurance is a great strategy to use to protect your loved ones against probate taxes. And depending on your circumstances and the type of policy you have, insurance may be used to increase or preserve wealth, and even to start or grow a new business. Walt Disney, for instance, used money from his whole life insurance policy to fund one of his amusement parks.

Some of the popular types of insurance that many people have and are familiar with are home, auto, and life insurance. Home and auto insurance may be able to preserve a home or a motor vehicle because of the potential replacement cost involved, but depending on the circumstances, the pay-out amount may not be sufficient to replace the vehicle or restore the home to the state prior to a misfortune. So, these types of insurance are not used to increase wealth. There are also other insurances, like short-term and long-term disability, and critical illness, which more people are buying these days, but they are more geared towards helping the insured when they are unable to work or function optimally in the work environment. Life insurance, however, may be used to increase wealth and grow a business. The two types that are useful are whole life and universal life insurance. How can these be used to increase wealth?

Whole Life Insurance

Whole life insurance is a permanent life insurance that will cover the insured until he dies. A whole life policy has a death benefit portion that is paid out to the beneficiary when the life insured dies, and it has an accumulated cash value that the policy holder will receive should he decide to surrender the policy. However, if the policy owner wants access to some of the cash value, but doesn't want to surrender the policy, he may borrow against the cash value, and repay the loan at a later time. Many entrepreneurs borrow funds against their whole life policies to fund or grow their businesses. When Walt Disney, for instance, needed funds to make Magic Kingdom the magical place it is today, he used his whole life policy to bankroll his venture so that his dreams could come true. Decades later, Magic Kingdom is the most visited theme park in the world, attracting more than 20 million visitors each year.

Some whole life policies also offer annual dividends. The policyholder may take these dividends in cash to increase his cashflow, or he may leave the dividend with the insurer to increase his cash value. This causes the cash value to grow at a faster rate, thus giving the owner access to more funds to borrow. The great news about borrowing from your policy is that it doesn't go on your credit history. It is viewed as a collateral loan, where the death benefit is the collateral. And if the policy owner is unable to repay the loan for whatever reason, it has no impact on his credit score. The insurer will recover the loan and interest accrued, from the death benefit when the life insured dies. So, the insurer will not realize any long-term loss. Maybe you were thinking about starting that Amazon business but had no idea where to get the funds. Perhaps your whole life policy is a good place to start looking.

Universal Life Insurance

Universal life insurance is a special kind of permanent insurance. It has an insurance component, and an investment savings component. This type of insurance was created because some people weren't very disciplined at saving. So, this gave them the option to have insurance for peace of mind as well as some savings to tap into when unexpected life events occur, for instance. Like the whole life policy, the insurance component has a death benefit that goes to the beneficiary when the life insured dies, while the investment savings portion accumulates a cash value. The investment earns interest as regular investments, and the interest earned is usually based on market conditions as with investments like mutual funds. This is the portion that can help you to increase wealth.

Premiums for a universal life policy may be paid as a lump sum or on a monthly basis. Monthly payment is more common because it's more affordable. When the premiums are paid, the insurance company will deduct an amount to cover the insurance portion— depending on the death benefit the policyholder chose—then the balance goes into an investment fund that attracts administration fees. The policyholder can determine how the funds are invested, so that he has control over the investment. And he can borrow or withdraw from the investment portion as required. However, like most investments, there are no guarantees, so there is a possibility for growth as well as decline in the investment component. For this reason, it is a good idea to do your research to make sound investment choices.

Also, since the investment portion grows tax-free—policyholders pay taxes on the growth only when the money is withdrawn—keep in mind that governments regulate these policies to prevent people from having too much money growing tax-free. Hence, there's a limit as to how much money you can put in the investment component. The rationale is that it is mainly an insurance instrument, so it should not be used predominantly for investment. Regardless, it is still a great instrument that can be used to increase wealth or to borrow money to grow that business you have been thinking about. In a later chapter, I will also share how borrowing from your life insurance policy can avoid the heavy weight of student loan debt around your children's necks.

Investing in Your Future

There are various ways to invest in your future, and I will be exploring a few in this section. Do keep in mind that whatever I share are just examples from my experiences. There are certainly other methods of investments that you could perhaps find more lucrative and successful. But it really doesn't matter which mode of investment that you choose, as long as you consider the type of lifestyle you want to live in the future, and you do the research to determine what kind of investment will help you to realize that lifestyle. Investing in your future could take one of the following forms:

1. Investing in education/coaching/mentoring that will help you to improve your future earnings
2. Investing in a business
3. Investing in a mutual or indexed fund
4. Investing in real estate
5. Investing in a retirement savings plan
6. Investing in a tax-free savings account

A sad fact is that many employees do not invest in their future beyond post-secondary education. They buy into the idea that going to school, getting good grades, and getting a good job will guarantee them a good lifestyle, even into retirement. And in some cases, that pans out well, depending on your profession and living expectations. But in many cases, people retire and get a rude awakening when they realize that there's not enough money to maintain the lifestyle they want after retirement.

There are also those employees who believe that the government will take care of them after retirement, by way of social security in the United States, and Canada Pension and old age security in Canada. Their companies have no automatic pension plan, like my Teachers' Pension Plan, for instance; and they do not invest in any individual retirement savings plan, like an IRA or an RRSP, where any worker can set up his or her own investment account. Unless you are planning to live poor after retirement, it is imperative that you invest in your future, and the earlier you start investing, the better lifestyle you'll enjoy later.

Investing in Education/Coaching/Mentoring

The education I'm referring to here is not the type you get from attending college. I'm referring to the education you get when your schooling ends. Many of us consider ourselves to be lifelong learners. But some of us fail to devote even the time to attend a free seminar to learn about new things. Watching television and going to the mall is more appealing. Some settle for mediocrity, and convince themselves they're not capable of achieving more. Everyone should invest in becoming a lifelong, self-directed learner, and continue to improve their God given talents, learning from reading books, listening to podcasts and webinars, attending seminars, and having a mentor or a coach to help you unlock your true potential and become the person God created you to become.

Investing in a Business

There are two ways to invest in a business. You can invest in your own business, and essentially become an entrepreneur. This could be a network marketing business that already has the systems in place for you, or it could be a start-up business of your own. The second way is to invest in someone else's business, which means becoming a shareholder in that business. Many companies, like Apple and Microsoft, use other peoples' money to cover start-up costs. Those people who invested, got shares in the company, meaning they own a part of the company. Later, when Apple and Microsoft went public and their stocks started trading on the stock exchange markets, these investors were able to sell their shares to realize enormous profits.

Investing in Real Estate

I believe real estate is one of the safest investments of all time, and it may be the safest one for the future. I don't think you can find a wealthy person who doesn't have real estate in his investment portfolio. Real estate can be residential or commercial, and you can be an active or passive real estate investor. Active real estate investors are usually landlords who manage their properties, whether directly or indirectly, through a property manager. A passive real estate investor usually puts up the money for the investment but is not actively involved with matters to do with the property. Profits are realized from monthly dividend payments or interest-only payments, and at the end of the investment period when the property is sold. Whether you want to be an active or a passive investor, there are many real estate investment opportunities available. Of course, always do your due diligence before you embark on any real estate investment venture.

Investing in a Retirement Savings Plan

Many employers of larger companies in the United States have a retirement plan for their employees, called a 401K. In Canada, companies offer an analogous retirement plan, called a group registered retirement savings plan (RRSP). Companies offering employees 401K or group RRSP usually set up and offer the plan to its employees. However, usually the employees cannot decide how the funds should be invested. Some companies will also match their workers' contributions to a specified limit. If you don't think you have the necessary skills to invest on your own, and you're not willing to take the time to learn, you should at least participate in a group retirement savings plan. There are also some additional benefits to participating in these plans.

1. The contributions you make in a retirement savings plan are tax-deferred. Income tax is charged only when you withdraw the money.
2. The contributions are used to reduce your income, which potentially leads to a tax refund, and that refund can be invested or used to pay down your debt.
3. If your income after retirement is less than your regular income, your retirement savings will be taxed at a lower rate then.
4. The money is automatically taken from your pay, so since you don't see it, there's no chance for you to spend it.

You also have the option to open an individual retirement savings account. In the United States, this is called an individual retirement account (IRA), while in Canada, it is called an individual RRSP. Anyone over 18 years can open one of these accounts, even if you're self-employed. In fact, if you're self-employed, this is an excellent way to reduce your taxable earnings.

Investing for your future is one of the most important things you can do. At least it gives you peace of mind that you'll be fine during your post-retirement years. The mistake many people make is waiting too late to start investing for retirement. But the earlier you start investing, the longer you can take advantage of deferred taxes, and the more you can take advantage of the compounding interest effect. If you're unsure of how to proceed, you can speak with a knowledgeable investor, like me, to learn more about investment strategies for investing in your future. In the next chapter, I will discuss how I came to realize that my financial IQ wasn't as high as I thought, what I did when I realized that I needed more financial education, the changes I made when I acquired a higher level of financial intelligence, and the impact that these changes had on my life and that of my family.

7
I Realized I Needed Financial Education

"If you want to thrive in today's economy, you must challenge the status quo and get the financial education necessary to succeed."

—Robert Kiyosaki

I Thought I Knew Enough

While growing up with my grandparents, who were farmers and had other small businesses, I learned about the importance of having multiple streams of income, from an early age. My grandfather taught me that saving should be a regular practice in my daily life. He would often say: "It's important to put away something for rainy days because you never know when they will come." At the time, I took my granddad's statement as another wise saying, because much of what he said during teachable moments was inundated with wise words. In retrospect, I do wonder if he meant "rainy days" literally, because he was a farmer. I have seen my grandfather's crops destroyed from flooding and continuous rainfalls. During such times, my grandparents relied on their other sources of income. Because I was quick with numbers and calculations, my grandparents included me in the running of their business, once I was old enough to understand and be of some assistance.

That, coupled with the fact that I was a strong math student, led me to believe that I knew enough about money and personal finance. I was a great saver, and I always strived to have something put away for rainy days. My grandfather's words, and my experiences, were first and foremost, and I tried to practice what he taught me about personal finance as I went about my daily life. After I had my first son, however, it didn't take too long for me to realize that my basic household income, and investment accounts in money market funds, weren't going to cut it. It became very clear that Richard and I needed to do more to increase our wealth to be able to raise our son the way we wanted to, and to save for our retirement to live the lifestyle we desired.

At that time, traditional high school education wasn't free in Jamaica, and parents had to purchase their children's textbooks. Although some secondary schools were either free or highly subsidized by the government, most parents preferred that their children attend the traditional high schools (where a school fee is paid to attend). What's the rationale here? Many parents believed their children would have received a higher level of education in these schools, rather than at the secondary schools. The perception was the same for primary and preparatory schools. Parents believed that the education received at a preparatory school—a private elementary school with a high fee—was better than that obtained at a public primary school, where no school fee was paid. So those who were able to afford it, preferred that their children attend a preparatory school, which can be very costly. No doubt my first son would have attended a preparatory school if we hadn't immigrated to Canada. When we left Jamaica, he was only three years old, and he was already attending a private school.

When Richard and I took stock of the cost it would have taken to give our son a proper education, we felt somewhat overwhelmed. With the economic climate in Jamaica at the time, and the limited opportunities that we foresee would be available for our son, we decided to capitalize on the opportunity to migrate to Canada. Based on our research, we concluded that Canada had a great education system, and that with its positive economic climate, it would have afforded our son better opportunities for greater success in his life. So, although I dreaded the minus twenty degrees temperatures that frequent Canada, it didn't take much convincing for me to agree to make the move. I kept believing that Canada had a great education system, for more than a decade. And during that time, I felt very proud to be part of this stellar education system, because I was helping to impact young people's lives, and setting them on the path for great success.

However, within the past eight years, the more I help Richard in our property management company, to do background checks to qualify tenants for residency, the more it dawns on me that the education system in Canada is falling short when it comes to setting up students for real-life success. Eventually, I became more concerned that I too was falling short in relation to setting up my students for great success in the future. It became apparent that too much emphasis was being placed on academics and the more abstract concepts that students have difficulty understanding, instead of on skilled jobs, entrepreneurship, and the importance of financial education. Everyone uses money, has to do personal finance, and needs financial education to have financial success, and yet financial education is missing from Canada's high school curriculum. So, my question to you is: Is an education system without financial literacy really that great?

A Wake-Up Call

It is possible that the financial knowledge I gained from my childhood days, and what I learned vicariously as I grew into adulthood, would have been sufficient had I stayed in Jamaica, but some of the rules regarding conducting financial affairs, in Canada and America, are very different from those in Jamaica. For instance, when I lived in Jamaica, I never had to file my taxes at the end of the year, like employees do in Canada and America. Every year, I would pay my taxes, and that was that. If my employers didn't ensure the appropriate taxes were deducted, then it was the government's bad luck. Credit bureaus and credit history didn't exist there either, and there was also no concept of a credit score, so I didn't need to have credit to purchase a car or a home. At the time, the mortgage term in Jamaica was the same as the amortization period, so the interest rate was fixed for the life of my mortgage. I didn't have to negotiate a new mortgage rate, or renew my mortgage after 3, 5, or 10 years, like in Canada. So, my mortgage payments were fixed for the life of the mortgage, since market conditions didn't affect existing mortgages, just new ones.

As a new immigrant in Canada, I initially felt I was at a disadvantage where financial literacy was concerned. And at the time, I believed it was because all my formal education prior to then, was done in Jamaica. I remember feeling the same way when I was in the United States as an undergrad student, trying to purchase that cellphone in Circuit City. Do you recall the story I shared in the previous chapter, about the salesperson who asked for my social security number to check my credit history? A few years after living in Canada, however, I realized that it wasn't just me, and it had nothing to do with where I did my education. Many Canadians were at a disadvantage too, because it became apparent that many people had a lower financial IQ than I did. And while I went on a self-directed learning journey to learn more, some people are just complacent with what they know, and refuse to research things for themselves. They prefer to ask a friend or family member, who is often as clueless as they are, but who love to provide advice from hearsay.

One of the criteria for sponsoring yourself and family to migrate to Canada is that you have to arrive with a large sum of money. At least it seemed very large at the time, considering the exchange rate was about thirty Jamaican dollars to one Canadian dollar. Don't quote me on this, but I believe then (the year 2000), I had to come with about $15,000 (Canadian) for my family of three. Richard was lucky to land a job before he came, and his income could cover all the household expenses. Thus, we invested some of the money in a mutual fund and left the rest in a savings account. We had no knowledge about mutual funds, but the advisor at Royal Bank made us believe we were making a good investment. We weren't accustomed to watching our investments, so we just invested and assumed it would grow over time, according to what we were told. But not paying attention to your investments can be very costly most times.

After the attack on the World Trade Center, on September 11, 2001, interest rates started to decline, and I got curious about the mutual fund performance. Much to my surprise, when I checked, the investment had dropped significantly below the original principal. A closer look made me realize that the decline in the recent months was also due to the fees that were being deducted, even though the fund was no longer performing. Upon reflection, it occurred to me that I really needed more financial education on investing. Listening to a financial advisor's recommendations wasn't safe, especially since I was ignorant about the investment class he advised me to purchase. A few years later, after learning and understanding more about mutual funds, I decided that mutual funds weren't my preferred way of investing. Thereafter, I still put some of the funds in a different mutual fund, which showed better performance and had a front-load fee, but I put most of the money in guaranteed investment certificates (GIC). The returns on GICs weren't great, but I loved that we knew exactly what we would be getting upon maturity. I also loved that my principal was safe, and I didn't have to check whether the value of the investment was increasing or decreasing.

The following year, we got a reality check. My first son's wish for a baby brother came true in May, and then a few months later, Richard got laid off from his job. How bizarre was that? Richard was unemployed, and I had one extra mouth to feed. During that time, we discussed the need to look at better investing strategies because we now had two children to send to university; plus, him not having a job became a reality for us. Fortunately for me, I had become a contract teacher with the Toronto District School Board by that time, so my colleagues assured me that the probability of me getting laid off was close to 0%. That gave me peace of mind. But not being comfortable with the unknown, I decided to cut my maternity leave short and return to full-time work.

While that was heartening, we still thought we needed to do more. We considered the stock market, but after some research and discussion, we felt that investing in the stock market would be like gambling, and we didn't have the heart for gambling. So, we kept most of our funds in GICs, capitalizing on credit card balance transfer promotions with 0% transfer fee and 0% interest rate. I will explain this strategy in more detail in the next chapter, but this is considered infinite returns because I was pocketing interest from funds that weren't mine.

I continued to use these strategies to increase my investment earnings for a few years, and when my second son was older, I started doing night school and summer school to increase my earnings. Within the same period, Richard began to do videos for weddings and events. Before long, however, it became apparent that we were working much harder, but our bank accounts weren't reflective of the additional work we were putting in. So evidently, the sacrifices we were making, and the time we were taking away from our family didn't seem justified. The more we earned, the more taxes we paid, so it appeared the government was reaping more benefits from our increased efforts. To add insult to injury, after the market crashed in 2008, and interest rates started to fall, GICs weren't attractive anymore, and the returns on our investments were depressing. So, we decided we needed some radical change.

The Effect of Change

Fortunately for me, some of my GICs were slated to mature in 2010 and 2011, so I still realized the 4 or 5 percentage return that I'd locked into, 3 or 4 years prior. Once those GICs matured, however, GICs weren't attractive anymore, and I immediately knew we had to change our investment strategies if we wanted to fund our children's education, live a good lifestyle after retirement, and still leave a legacy for them. So Richard and I were frequently at the investment discussion table deciding on our next step.

During that time, we also decided to sell our home in Jamaica. We had concluded that going back home was a remote possibility, and even if we did, we wouldn't want to live in the same area. With the low mortgage rates in 2009, and not receiving much interest on our investments, we decided to move to a larger home so that the boys would have more space whenever their friends came over to play. What did we have to lose when a low-interest rate was in our favour to buy a bigger home? We already saw how much our home in Jamaica had appreciated over the years, and the returns we got from selling. Plus, we could have bought a much bigger house in Canada, and the mortgage payments were close to what we were paying for our townhome.

Because of the market uncertainty, Richard wasn't one hundred percent on board to purchase a bigger home. He was worried that interest rates would rise soon after, and our mortgage payment could double. But he'll be the first to tell you that I can be as stubborn as a mule when I make up my mind to do something. The decision to purchase a bigger home at that time was one of the best decisions I've made in my life. In late 2009, when I couldn't find a home meeting my expectations, I told my realtor that we would stop looking and would wait for the new year to see what was in store. In January 2010, she called me and shared that she had the ideal home I was looking for, although the price was above what I'd stipulated. I trusted my realtor, however, so we went to look at the home. When the owners opened the door, I fell in love with the home immediately. Luckily for us, the owners wanted a June 28th closing, and since we were in no hurry, we worked out a deal. We all gave a bit to make the deal work, and that included my realtor too—in retrospect, it seemed that all the stars were aligned.

The extended closing date gave Richard and me multiple opportunities to visit the investment discussion table, and multiple opportunities to talk to my Lord and Saviour about showing me the possibilities to make my decision work for the greater good of my family. My prayers and pleading didn't go in vain. During the March Break, my sisters came and helped me prepare our home to put it on the market. I told my realtor that I only wanted her to do the viewing, because I didn't relish having realtors that I didn't know taking people into my home. After a few viewings, we got two offers. We were in the process of negotiating the better offer when I had an epiphany… or maybe it was the voice of God that spoke to me…*Don't sell the townhome, Ingrid*.

Richard was fast asleep when I had the epiphany, and I must have shaken him about five times before he came awake. When I thought he was alert enough, I told him that we weren't going to sell our townhome. He looked at me as though I'd grown two horns, and he said that I should just go back to bed because I was dreaming and talking crazy. After sharing that I wasn't sleeping but was wide-awake thinking, and after I reiterated that we were not going to be selling our home, he looked even more intently at me, like I had grown 10 more horns. When he realized that I wasn't going to quit, he asked: *Are you crazy? I'm here thinking that buying a bigger home could cause us more expenses, and now you're thinking about having two homes?* Like I shared above, I can be as stubborn as a mule when I decide to do something. So, in 2010, our real estate journey began, and now, nine years later, we still have our original townhome, plus homes in 8 other cities in Ontario, Canada, and in the United States.

I knew before I started investing in real estate that it is a safer investment, and one that would help me to build wealth for my family. Why? Because many of the wealthy people I read about had real estate in their portfolios. Moreover, my bank wouldn't allow me to transfer money—even temporarily—from my LOC to buy a mutual fund in my tax-free savings account, but I had no issue getting multiple mortgages. At the time, it didn't make sense, because I only wanted to transfer $10,000 until I got home, yet my two mortgages were more than $500,000. The answer became apparent when I read the book, *Rich Dad Poor Dad,* by Robert Kiyosaki. I learned from Robert that the bank won't lend you money to buy mutual funds because they are risky investments, but the bank loves to give mortgages because they are safer investments.

Although I'd improved my financial literacy skills over the years, by perusing the internet, attending some seminars, and reading books, because school didn't teach me financial education, I had to embark on self-directed learning activities to increase my financial IQ even more. Since books like the *Rich Dad Poor Dad* series stressed that a high financial education is paramount if I wanted to be a successful real estate investor, I started to read more books on finances and real estate, listen to podcasts, and engage in investors' networking groups; I also attended presentations, seminars, and workshops. As time progressed, I realized that the more I learned, the more I came across things that I wanted to learn more about. So, I paid to attend classes to learn from the experts, like *Rich Dad Poor Dad* teachers, and Tom and Nick Karadza—the "Rock Star" brothers—from Rock Star Real Estate. As time went by, I included webinars and networking meetups to the list of media that was helping me to increase my knowledge. And I keep learning new things every day, from audiobooks, podcasts, YouTube videos and much more.

Why A⁺ in Math ≠ Financial Literacy

Throughout my teaching career, I've encountered many A⁺ students who were clueless when it came to matters about money. Some of them could factor a complex quadratic expression much faster than I could, but if I asked them a trivial question relating to money, they couldn't respond. This is a common question I've asked my grade 11 and 12 students: *Which of these have a lower interest rate—a credit card or a line of credit?* I rarely get the correct answer, and sometimes instead of a response, I get this question: *"Ms., what is a line of credit?"* And, even though I too was an A⁺ math student, the simple lessons in financial education that I learned from my grandparents, served me much better financially than all the A's I received in high school and university. I learned from my grandparents that having multiple streams of income is very important; I learned that starting to save from an early age, and owning my own home, is essential for financial success. I learned that money is not made for just spending, but for saving and multiplying to earn more. And I also learned that sharing my wealth with others who are in need, will store up blessings for me in heaven.

My grandparents didn't attend high school or college, but they obviously knew how to manage their money wisely. For instance, while my grandfather worked on the farm during weekdays, my grandmother managed a small grocery store. They would use proceeds from the farm to purchase items, not grown locally, from the market in Kingston to sell in the community market on weekends. The monies obtained from both ventures were then pumped into the grocery store, and this evolved into multiple sources of cashflow. At times, I questioned why it was important to my grandparents to have different modes for earning income, because fellow farmers in the community who focused on just farming appeared to be doing just fine. But one June, the realization hit me when disaster struck, and the answer became apparent.

Incessant rainfall had led to flooding in my childhood community, which wiped out many crops. Many farmers, including my grandparents, were badly affected. The impact on my family, however, was minimal compared to others, because mine had other sources of income, coupled with the fact that my grandparents had savings for "rainy days." My grandparents obviously had a high level of financial literacy—even though they weren't considered sophisticated investors—and they were entrepreneurs who possessed the necessary skills to manage their money effectively. Even though school failed to teach me financial education, the way my grandparents conducted their financial affairs impacted me from an early age, and it positively affected my mindset towards money later on in my life.

Once I began working and saving, trying to obtain multiple streams of income became one of my ongoing goals. Having a single source of income appeared rather risky. But as useful as those lessons were, they weren't enough. I learned later—especially after immigrating to Canada, away from family support—that I still needed to learn more about managing money. Moving to a country where I couldn't just leave my son with my neighbours and go to the food store, was a wake-up call. Coupled with that, at the time, kindergarten was only half a day. I'd lost the luxury of being able to pick up my son after my school ended, without having to pay for after-care. I remembered the cost for half-day after-care being so expensive, so it made more sense to have my son in a Montessori school all day, than in a public school where paying for before and after-care was necessary.

The Montessori fee was more than $800 per month, and it didn't include lunch. And that may not sound like a lot of dough now, but when starting over in a new country with the hopes of owning a home soon, saving the down payment for a home seemed very unlikely with such expenses. I'd already had my home in Jamaica, and I kept remembering my grandfather telling me that I should always strive to own my home, so that was always first and foremost in my mind. Hence, during all that time, I kept my eyes on my goal of owning my own home in Canada, and on improving my financial well-being and my family's as well. That, plus the turn in the economy after 9/11, took me on a journey and a quest to become more financially literate, and I went down different investment paths to achieve financial independence. School did not prepare me for any of this, and I kept wondering, if not in school, where are people supposed to learn about money management and personal finance?

Where You Should Learn Financial Literacy

If you ask the government in countries around the world this question: Who is responsible for educating the young people in your country? I believe, ninety-nine percent of the time, you will get the response: "We are." But what if you were to ask this question, around the world, instead: Mr. Government, have you financially educated your young people? What do you think the responses would be? Do you think you would get a "yes" more than one percent of the time you asked?

Many governments will share how much money they are investing in literacy and numeracy initiatives to equip teachers with the necessary skills to improve students' learning and performance in these areas, but how many are investing in programs to train teachers to teach financial education? Why is this? Could it be that governments don't think financial education is as important as literacy and numeracy?

I believe many people have no qualms spending money where they believe a great value lies, and I don't think governments are any different. In fact, many governments are guilty of wasting money on insignificant ventures that benefit neither them nor their residents. So they will waste tax payers' money on unwanted ventures, but using the public's funds to financially educate the masses so that they can acquire the knowledge and the skills to manage their money, stay out of debt, and build a strong financial foundation, doesn't seem to be at the top of governments' priority list. Why do you think this is?

Are they blinded to the debt crisis that looms over the world's economy, and are they blinded to the amount of consumer debt their residents are carrying? In Canada, the ratio of debt to disposable income is approaching 180 percent. This is up almost 30 percent from a decade earlier. In June of 2019, Equifax Canada reported that Canadians owe more than $1.9 trillion in consumer debt. And while this amount may seem low compared to other countries, when compared to Canada's population and its gross domestic product, that is the highest debt load in the Group of Eight economies. Figure 1.1 shows the household debt to gross domestic product for Canada and other G8 countries. Canada is performing the worst, at 100.2%; United Kingdom is next, at 86.5%; and then the US, at 76.4%.

Figure 1.1 Debt-Laden

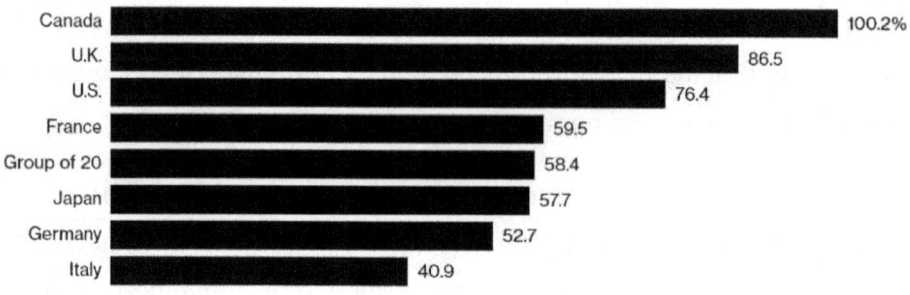

Source: **Bank of International Settlements**

Many Canadian and American households are feeling the crunch. The debt-service-ratio, which is a measure of how much disposable income goes towards paying the principal and interest for a loan, has climbed more than 15 percent in Canada and the US, from 2018 to 2019. And the ratio continues to climb, while more Canadians and Americans are filing for insolvency.

Although the debt to gross domestic product in the US is significantly lower than that in Canada, the debt situation in the US is even more gloomy. The consumer debt in the United States is more than $13.5 trillion. Many Americans are living in poverty although America is one of the wealthiest countries in the world. Even though Qatar is ranked the richest country globally, with a gross national income per capita of $116,799, and America ranks the twelfth richest country, with a gross national income per capita of $55,350, these numbers can be misleading. America has a population of 325 million people, while Qatar has only 2.6 million people. So, Qatar's population is less than 1% of that of America. If you were to calculate the gross national income for America and Qatar, you would see that America is sitting at almost $18 trillion, while Qatar is only at $304 billion.

Why are there so many poor people in such a rich country? A lack of financial education is at the top of the list of reasons. Most of the wealth is owned by 10% of America's population. And this 10% either have superior financial intelligence compared to the other 90%, or they surround themselves with advisors who have a very high financial IQ. Without financial education, these wealthy people and their advisors would not be able to hold onto the wealth. They would be like a lottery winner with no financial literacy, who winds up broke within a couple of years because they have no knowledge about managing money, or about how to make money work for them. Moreover, despite the wad of money they get from their winnings, some of these winners even end up filing for bankruptcy. Because, as I said in a previous chapter, *a fool and his money will soon be parted.*

I believe the word *"fool"* in that adage is referring to a financially illiterate person. Hence, putting it into perspective, the saying can be rephrased as: *A financially illiterate person and his money will soon be parted.* Money has it's own rules, and it doesn't stay with people who don't know how to preserve it and multiply it. Thus, it will not stay with you if you don't have financial education. And this is where governments are failing their citizens. They don't think financial education is valuable, so it is not taught in schools, and its importance is not emphasized the way literacy and numeracy are stressed. I do wonder sometimes if this is a deliberate strategy that governments use to prevent their citizens from prospering too much. Do they want to keep the wool over residents' eyes, so to speak, so they become slaves to the system instead of becoming emancipated financially successful individuals?

The Mistakes I Could Have Avoided

This sounds clichéd, but despite how many times I've heard that you learn more from taking action and making your own mistakes, I still share with people that as a real estate investor, some of my greatest learnings were bred from the mistakes that Richard and I made. But on the other hand, I also had great learnings from listening to people's stories, the mistakes that they made, and their advice as to how to safeguard myself to avoid them. But whether you're learning from your own or other people's mistakes, learning the landscape, in general, can make a whole lot of difference and save you a lot of grief when you embark on any new journey. I still do believe that some of my mistakes could have been avoided if I had learned more about investing in real estate, before I took the plunge to become a real estate investor. Plus, a higher level of financial intelligence may have helped me to realized higher gains in a shorter time. In addition, understanding people's mindset about money, and how a lack of financial education can negatively impact their decisions regarding finances, would have definitely caused me to be less emotional when selecting tenant applicants. This too would have saved us some unnecessary headaches in the earlier years of our investment venture.

Richard and I embarked on our real estate investing journey, feeling that we've been around the block a few times to be able to weather the storms. And while there were some truths to this, we ended up losing thousands of dollars because we needed more knowledge, skills, and ultimately more financial education. Besides, we needed to understand that people who have a track record of not being able to manage their money effectively because they lack financial literacy, will not suddenly be able to make sound financial decisions because they have a better job and getting more income. Parkinson's Law says expenditure will always rise to meet income. So people need financial education to change that track record and start on a new trajectory. All getting more income means to financial illiterate people is that they have more money to blow. And sometimes they seem to be in a race to discover if they can blow more money in a much shorter time.

For instance, a few years ago, I recommended giving a tenant a chance, who I knew was not an ideal one. All the writing was on the wall. The tenant's credit score was very low, her student loan was not being paid, and there wasn't enough money in her account to pay the first and last month's rent. However, I decided to give her a chance, for three reasons. For the purpose of explaining the situation, I will call the tenant, Jean.

One, Jean was able to borrow some money from a family member who was very supportive, and who believed that she had gotten her act together. Two, since Jean didn't think she was successful in the field she had studied before, she had gone back to school to pursue studies in a new field that she thought was more suitable for her, and that would have provided her with better income. Three, Jean had gotten employment in her new field, and even though at the time she was still on probation, she was making close to twice the amount of money than before, to cover her expenses.

All was well for the first few months, but before long, we started to receive notification from the city that the water bill was not being paid. After some talking to, Jean made partial payments towards the water bill. Then, eventually, the rent was returned because of insufficient funds. We suspended the preauthorized rent payment for her, and asked that the rent be sent by electronic transfer. Partial payments would be e-transferred to us, until one month no payment came. By checking in with the supportive family member, we learned that Jean had slipped back into her old ways, partying and not being responsible with her money, to name a few. Suffice to say, we had to evict Jean, and the whole process cost us a few thousand dollars.

What disappointed me most from this experience was the fact that this was a young individual who had some ambition, thought she could do more, and wanted better for herself. She saw her life at a point where she didn't want to be; she went back to school, putting herself in more student loan debt, thinking that she would improve her situation, but she ended up worse than where she was. She had more debt, and she eventually lost her job because she had slipped into a state of depression and wasn't arriving to work on time; plus, some days, she just didn't even turn up for work.

Of course, there are other contributing factors to the outcome of this situation, but do you think things could have turned out differently for this individual if she had been financially educated? Definitely! I could share more money-related actions that resulted in the undesired outcome, but that is not necessary. The point here is that a lack of financial education can break people's resolve and prevent them from attaining their dreams. And not knowing the impact that financial illiteracy can have on your clients, can negatively impact the decisions you make in your business, which can ultimately affect your bottom line.

Many of us grow up hearing that saving is important, but how many of us were taught how to really save? This and other experiences and stories that I've listened to from tenant applicants and some of my past students, spurred me to write this book on the importance of teaching financial education in school. A lack of financial education is an epidemic that is affecting our young people, and if something is not done about it, many of them will not be successful in the future. Bad spending habits and bad financial decisions that lead to bad debt, poor credit scores, and even bankruptcy, could soon become the norm, and if this happens, our countries' economies will be in a dreadful state of economic affairs for the future. Join me in the next chapter, where I'll share about some of the things I learned, and the opportunities I capitalized on, as I journeyed on my mission to become financially intelligent. The knowledge you'll glean from my experience will definitely change your mindset, and cause you to start thinking outside the box when it comes to money.

8

My Journey to Become Financially Intelligent

"Because financially capable consumers ultimately contribute to a stable economic and financial system, as well as improve their own financial situations, it's clear that the Federal Reserve has a significant stake in financial education."

—Ben Bernanke

I Learned More Outside the Classroom

Learning is a lifelong activity and, over the years, I came to the realization that the classroom is just the beginning of our learning journey. Most of the useful knowledge that I use in my daily life— when I'm not teaching—I learned from self-directed learning activities and attending informal learning events. Although I'm a high school math teacher, I honestly cannot even say university prepared me for my job, because the math I learned in university is very different from high school math. University math was mostly about proving theorems, corollaries, lemmas, and more. There were times when I felt like I was proving all the things that I was already using for years, such as why x plus negative x is equal to zero. I will definitely give some credit to teachers college, because that was where I was introduced to things such as child psychology, the psychology of learning, teaching methodologies, and classroom behaviour and management strategies. These learnings help me in not only my teaching profession, they also help me to raise my two boys. My master's program was also very useful, especially since I had a community of likeminded people who were already in the teaching profession and sharing their lived experiences.

In fact, if it wasn't for my master's program, perhaps I wouldn't have gotten the courage to write this book. As I mentioned before, I'm a numbers person, so being a good writer was never my thing. My grade 11 English teacher, especially, would stress how clumsy some of my sentences were, and how I would write the way I speak, which is not the proper way for good writers. It was also very evident when she returned my work, which had red ink all over it. I had heard and seen the evidence so often that eventually I just accepted that I would never be a writer—let alone a good one. So as long as I scored enough to pass English Language, I was satisfied. My master's in education program was centered on writing posts and academic papers, however, and I knew from day one that I had to improve my writing skills if I wanted commendable results. As it was fully online, a great chunk of my mark came from posting in the discussion forums, and all 10 courses had at least two major writing assignments.

There were two courses where we had to do peer editing, and my goodness, was I petrified? One of my professors assured me that I had nothing to worry about because, had I not shared, she would have had no idea that my undergrad studies were in math and computer science. It wasn't very reassuring, but it certainly helped to calm my nerves. And upon further reflection, I felt like my writing skills had indeed improved, from emailing, posting, and journaling. The feedback I received from my peers was surprisingly positive, and I received A's on both papers.

Because of the confidence I'd gained from those experiences, I mustered the courage to later share with one of my professors about my desire to write about the importance of teaching young people financial literacy. She was very excited to hear that I wanted to help people in that capacity, even though it meant that I would be doing something that pushed me out of my comfort zone. Her final comments were that I shouldn't give up, that I have what it takes to do it, and that she hoped to have that book in her hand one day. Her words kept playing over and over in my head, despite the countless times that I said, *"Yeah, right!"*

But she was like that teacher you never forgot, because they did or said that one special thing that served as a motivating factor for you—that teacher who, even though school ended several moons before, is always front and foremost in your mind. And at every step of your life's journey, you keep replaying that one incident or that one conversation over and over again. Have you ever had such a teacher? I was very lucky to have one, even later in my life, when I had a mission to bring to fruition. She gave me the courage to act on my dream, and I went on a learning expedition to take action to pursue my mission and realize my goal. Hence, my first call of duty, after I get copies of my book, is to post one to Professor Randee Lawrence. So, if you're now reading my book, the seed that Professor Randee planted while I was in the academic space, has led to my growth outside the classroom.

The Difference Between a Job and Making Money

A lot of people believe going to school and getting good grades will land you a job that will cover living expenses, with enough left over to cover recreation and investing for retirement. I too, believed that for a very long time. The sad truth is, with the high cost of living, many employees do not earn enough money to cover all their expenses and then some. The average household income in both Canada and the United States is less than $50,000. Most families are currently spending more on rent or mortgage payments than the thirty percent that experts recommend they should be paying. Many are using credit cards to supplement their living. But if they become unemployed for a month or two, things can quickly become very dismal for them. How can this be prevented?

It is important for you to know the difference between having a job and having the means to make money. The rich and affluent focus on making money, while the poor and middle class are more concerned about getting a job. Many people believe that when they have a job, they are making money, because they receive a paycheck at the end of each pay cycle. Having a job, however, only allows you to earn money because you have to use your skills and trade your time and effort daily to receive remuneration at the end of the week or month. However, this is not considered making money, because if you decided to stop trading your time and using your energy one week, you would not be paid for that week. Making money doesn't require you to keep sacrificing your time and effort to be paid. You make money when the one or two sacrifices you made today, generates income for the future, with no further effort required on your part.

People also view a job as a ticket to their retirement. And while this may be true for some jobs that have a defined benefit pension plan, that is not the case for many jobs in today's market. A defined benefit pension plan is too expensive for employers to sustain in the current economic climate, so more and more companies are opting to match employees' 401K or RRSP contributions instead. As a result, when employees retire, the company is not liable for funding their retirement, and if market conditions result in low performing retirement savings plans, the company is not responsible for any topping up to supplement their retirees' income.

There are several ways to make money, but sadly, these methods are not shared with you in school. School teaches you to become employees to earn money, instead of teaching you techniques to increase your cashflow. Here is a list of some of the strategies that many entrepreneurs utilize to make money:

1. Investing in a rental property that gives monthly cashflow
2. Building a parking lot where people pay to park every day
3. Composing popular music that is used regularly
4. Writing a book and getting royalties each time it is sold
5. Writing a book that a film company turns into a movie
6. Doing a painting that is printed and sold multiple times

This list is not exhaustive, but I'm sure you get the idea. If you develop strategies to make money, you will make money even when you're sleeping. In fact, all the examples listed above will cause your estate to continue making money even when your time on Earth has expired. Many affluent people continue to enjoy the finer things in life without continuing to work, because of the sacrifices they made yesterday to ensure that they keep making money in the future. Hence, these examples are classified as assets that will provide you with multiple streams of income. And with various streams of income, you will be in a better position to achieve financial independence and live a better lifestyle before and after retirement.

Assets Vs Liability

What is an asset and what is a liability? How can you easily distinguish between the two? Put simply, an asset is something that puts money in your pocket, while a liability is anything that takes money out of your pocket. Many people confuse a liability for an asset, and for this reason, they buy more liabilities than they do assets. The high consumer household debt that exists in many countries can be attributed to the lack of knowledge regarding these two terms. If consumers understand the difference between an asset and a liability, this may cause them to make better choices when it comes to spending.

For instance, many people will purchase a new car because they believe it will have more value. What they may not realize is that a car starts losing its value the moment it's driven from the dealership. Hence, a week later, their new car will be valued less than its purchased price. Plus, there are other expenses associated with owning a car, such as insurance, license, gas, and maintenance costs, which clearly indicates that a car takes money from your pocket; therefore, it is definitely a liability.

Some liabilities may be considered an asset, however, because they may also put money in your pocket. An Uber driver, for instance, uses his car to earn money. So, although there are expenses associated with owning the car, because it produces cash flow from each trip, for that use, it is considered an asset as well. Your home is another example of an asset and a liability. When Robert Kiyosaki wrote, in *Rich Dad Poor Dad,* that your personal home was a liability, many people thought he didn't know what he was talking about because most people viewed their home as their greatest asset.

However, after the 2008 housing crash in the United States, which saw many homeowners with mortgages that were greater than the values of their homes, it became apparent that Robert knew what he was talking about. There are many costs involved in owning a home, such as a mortgage, home insurance, property tax, maintenance costs, and appliance replacement costs. As long as you're living in the home and paying these expenses, it is a liability to you. Even if the home appreciates in value and you have no mortgage, it is still considered a liability, because you still have to pay your property taxes, and cover maintenance expenses. However, it could also be an asset if you decide to rent a part of it, or if you were to sell it and the selling price was greater than your mortgage balance.

Good Debt vs Bad Debt

One day, I asked my students to share in a word cloud what came to mind when they heard the word "debt." Here are some of the responses I got:

- Bankruptcy
- Broke
- Depressed

- No Money
- Screwed
- In Trouble

I didn't get even one positive response. If I were to ask you to share what comes to your mind, what words would you share? Would they be very different from my students' words, or pretty much the same?

Many people view debt as a bad thing, and there is even a certain stigma attached to the word "debt." So much so that some people don't even like talking about it if they fell victim to it, and they would never admit that they are in debt. But while it may be possible to live completely debt-free, it is not necessarily the wisest choice. Having debt can be a very good thing, depending on the type of debt we're talking about.

There are two types of debt: good and bad. Good debt is usually used for investments that put money in your pocket over the long run, and helps you to increase your wealth. Bad debt is a burden, and it takes money out of your pocket. An example of bad debt is the debt you incur from buying liabilities. Good debt usually attracts a lower interest rate, and depending on what you use the debt to do, the interest may be tax-deductible.

For instance, Richard and I have a property management company that manages some of our investment properties, and some for fellow investors. We used zero percent balance transfers on our credit card to start up the management company, and we borrowed money in the form of mortgages to purchase our investment real estate. We also used funds from our line of credit for the down payment for some of the properties. All the mortgage interest, and any interest that accrues on the credit card are tax-deductible because they are used for business purposes.

The benefits on these loans are two-fold as well. Apart from the tax break on the interest, over time, the value of the property management company increased as the number of properties managed rose. Also, the value of our properties appreciates every year. Once enough equity was built up in the properties, from mortgage paydown and appreciation, we refinanced them and used the money to pay off the line of credit. This gave us access to more funds, which we reused to purchase more real estate, thus increasing our property holdings. This is actually why all debt is not considered bad. In fact, this strategy is so awesome, it helped us to realize gains that we would never have obtained if we were waiting to save enough funds to purchase more real estate, or to start the management company.

It is consumer debt—the debt people use to buy things that they can definitely do without—that is considered bad. Sometimes the things bought are thrown out long before they can afford to pay them off. They use credit cards and loans to buy things that they do not need, often because of impulses and emotions, and frequently because of the need to compete with or impress people they don't even like. If you can share why people perpetually put themselves in debt to present a false image of themselves, or to impress people they can't stand to be in a room with sometimes, do share!

And I'm not bashing all consumer debts; sometimes circumstances—such as loss of a job, death of a loved one, and job relocation—require that you take on some consumer debt. Why? Because I don't believe you should take money from your savings every time unexpected expenses come up. A consumer loan can help to care for yourself or your family while you relocate or seek new employment. It could be used to purchase a plane ticket to attend a funeral, or to help family members cover funeral expenses. I too had to take on some consumer debt over the years, but these debts have always been for short periods. And where possible, I usually use my credit card first, to capitalize on the grace period, which gives me a longer time before interest starts to accrue. And if I'm unable to pay off my credit card, I use my line of credit to cover the balance because the interest rate is much lower. Thereafter, I cut back on some spending where possible so that I can clear the loan as fast as possible. The lesson here is that a consumer debt should be taken as a means to an end, and your intentions should be to repay them as fast as you're able to.

I want to emphasize that in situations where unexpected life events cause you to borrow money, you should always opt for the lower interest loan, like lines of credit. They usually attract the prime interest rate plus a percentage add-on that is dependent on your credit score. This is another reason why maintaining a good credit score is very beneficial. I have seen credit card interest rates range from a low of 9% to a high of 29%. And there is inconsistency among different cards, even for those cards issued by the same lending institution. Thus, it is crucial that you know the rate on all your cards. If you don't have a line of credit—of course, my suggestion is that everyone should have one—and you must use your credit card for emergency reasons, use the card with the lowest interest rate.

If you have only one credit card, you may be saying: *But I only have one card, so what do I do?* In that case, you have no choice, but I believe everyone who is educated to use credit cards effectively shouldn't have just one. Additional cards give you more opportunities to capitalize on the grace period each card offers, and it allows you to split payments over different pay cycles. The story I shared in a previous section about my microwave dying unexpectedly after the Christmas Holidays, reiterates why using only one credit card is not necessarily beneficial, even when that card gives you the highest reward points. The takeaway here, however, is that consumer debt attracts higher interest rates, and the interest accrues is certainly not tax-deductible. So, the longer you have them, the more they hurt your bottom line, and the longer you will be in debt.

Here are some examples of good and bad debts:

Good Debt

- Mortgages – homes usually appreciate in value
- Business start-up loans – most successful businesses start with even shareholders loans
- Car loans – if the car helps to put money in your pocket
- Student loan – if it provides knowledge to put money in your pocket
- Loans to purchase precious metals that keep their value or appreciates
- Loans for investments that yield a greater rate of return

Bad Debt

- Loans to purchase consumer items like clothes, shoes, furniture, and electronic gadgets
- Car loans – if the car doesn't put money in your pocket
- Payday loans
- Credit card cash advance – if the rate is not a low promotional one
- Vacation loans – if you don't see yourself paying off the balance soon

How I Made Money from Credit Cards

The credit card is one of the best inventions ever! But like anything else, if you don't know how to use it effectively, it can be viewed in a negative light. But answer this question for me: Where can you get a loan every month at 0% interest rate for the duration of your billing period and grace period—at least 51 days for most cards. You pay interest only if you don't repay the balance in full by the bill due date.

And I know you're already asking: Really? ... Can I actually make money from credit cards? The answer is, yes you can! I have been using credit cards to make money since the year 2004, and if you didn't think that was possible, it is time to really listen and learn so that you can start doing it too.

Before the year 2004, I used to get credit card applications in the mail that had 0% interest and a 0% balance transfer fee for 12 months. Of course, at that time, I had a lower financial IQ, and I was brainwashed to think that having too many credit cards was bad, so I would immediately recycle the offers. In 2004, I received an offer that said I was preapproved for $20,000, and I could do a 0% balance transfer for 12 months at 0% interest. Twenty thousand dollars sounded like a lot of money, so I kept that application. Plus, at that time, I had been living in Canada for only four years, and the two credit cards I had were joint, with Richard as the primary owner, and I thought how wonderful it would be to have a card of my own. I applied for the card and, as stated, my limit was $20,000.

Nowadays, most credit card companies charge a fee for balance transfers, but in 2004, there were no balance transfer fees involved. And at that time, interest rates were higher. So I took a balance transfer of $19,900 from the credit card, and put it on a one-year GIC, at 5% interest, in ING Direct, now called Tangerine. Each month, I paid the minimum balance—interest rate was 0%, so it didn't matter—and at the end of the year, I cashed the GIC to pay back the credit card balance. The interest of $995 was mine, at no cost to me. That was an infinite return, because the $19,900 was borrowed money.

I did this several times with multiple credit cards, and even when interest rates plummeted in 2008, there were still benefits. I would have realized greater benefits too, if I wasn't closing some of the cards after the promotion ended. What I later learned, thanks to a rep at Maryland Bank (MBNA), who discouraged me from closing the credit card, was that if I kept the account opened, another promotion would eventually come. Her advice was instrumental in starting our real estate investment journey.

In 2010, when I decided my boys needed a study room, away from the distraction of the game and the TV in their rooms, I used the balance transfer from the MBNA credit card to help with the closing cost for a new home, because I decided to not sell our townhome. I can't remember if a loan fee was in effect by then, but it didn't matter because my promotion was zero percent for 15 months, and it was worth it. Before the 15 months was up, I refinanced the townhome that had appreciated more than $100,000 after one year, on top of the equity that had accrued since we bought it in 2002. Hence, I had enough to pay back the credit card balance, and purchase three more properties, by the end of 2012. That was when my real estate investment journey really began.

Since interest rates are much lower now, and credit cards sometimes have a loan fee that is greater than the bank's GIC rates, I no longer use balance transfers to buy GICs, but I've used them for short-term private loans. These loans are usually 6 to 8%, better rates than even the GIC I purchased in 2004. I also use the balance transfers to reduce the amount of interest I pay on my business-related loans and my business lines of credit. For instance, if my business line of credit is 6%, and I get a balance transfer for zero percent for 15 months, with a loan fee of 2%, I would save more than 4% on interest because that 2% is a one-time fee that covers a zero percent payment for more than one year.

Using Other People's Money to Build Wealth

The examples I shared in the previous section, which illustrate how I've been using credit cards, lines of credits, and mortgages, for the past 15 years, to invest and do business to make more money, are exemplars of how you can use other people's money (OPM) to build wealth. Unless you were born with a gold spoon in your mouth, as my grandfather would say to indicate that you were born well off, it's much easier to grow wealth using OPM than it is to save your own money to accumulate wealth. Despite being a great saver, when I took stock of all the funds Richard and I had saved up to 2005, 5 years after we came to Canada, I realized that if we didn't have some savings from Jamaica, we still would not have had enough money to pay down 20% on the home that we had purchased three years prior.

Why were you thinking about a 20% down payment on a home that you already own, you might be asking?

Well, that home cost $250,000 at the time, and in an effort to not deplete all our savings, we opted for a 10% down payment. Even though we could have afforded up to 17%, we figured that down payment made more sense. But why? In Canada, any mortgage that is more than 80% of the home purchase price is considered a high-risk mortgage. And every high-risk mortgage attracts an insurance premium that is added to the cost of the home. Of course, that didn't sit well with me because I felt like all that did was increase the purchase price of the house. However, the difference between the premium at 10% and 15% wasn't a significant saving, so we figured having more money in our pockets after closing made more sense. But I still used to wonder how long it would have taken us to have the $50,000 down payment so our mortgage didn't attract a premium.

When I purchased my second home, in 2010, I used up pretty much all of our savings, except for what was in our retirement savings plan. In fact, I was still short to cover the transfer taxes and other closing costs without additional help. It was my dear father-in-law who came to my rescue. I was determined to not sell my townhome, and I was determined to pay 20% down so that I wouldn't have a high-risk mortgage. So, I reached out to my father-in-law even when Richard felt it was too weird to ask his own dad for help. And when Richard complained that it felt too risky moving into a home that was more than twice the size of the townhome, which meant taxes and utilities would be double what we used to pay, I capitalized on a promotional 0% balance transfer on my MBNA credit card. I figured it would be a safety net for us until the dust settled.

Our expenses for the new home had almost doubled indeed, which meant I had far less money to save than I was able to prior to moving. So, if in 2010, I'd started to save for the down payment to purchase more investment properties, there's absolutely no way I could have bought those three homes I purchased in 2012. Moreover, apart from the three homes in Canada, I had also bought a townhouse in foreclosure in Lake Mary, Florida. Were it not for OPM, I wouldn't have had enough money two years later to purchase even one of these homes. Perhaps, even nine years later, the time of writing this paragraph, I would only have one additional property, and maybe none, since the prices appreciated significantly in the Greater Toronto Area after 2010.

So today, I have a real estate portfolio that was predominantly funded by other people's money. All my investment properties and my primary residence were purchased with the help of the bank. Some of my other investments were also initially funded with OPM, until I gradually repaid the loans over time. Thus, I've been primarily using OPM to increase my wealth for the past 15 years. Without a strong financial education, however, using other people's money can be very risky. I'm a normal person just like you, but OPM and financial education are responsible for putting me in the financial position I'm in today.

If you don't feel like you're there yet, you can definitely achieve your financial goals by becoming financially educated, and using some of the same strategies that I've outlined above! And now that you have heard some of my stories as I travelled on my journey to increase my financial IQ and improve my financial foundation, keep on reading to learn about the great things I've accomplished after becoming more financially intelligent.

9

What I Accomplished After Becoming Financially Literate

"Learning is the beginning of wealth. Learning is the beginning of health. Learning is the beginning of spirituality. Searching and learning is where the miracle process all begins."

—Jim Rohn

Increasing My Assets and Limiting My Liabilities

The two most important lessons I learned from becoming more financially intelligent are: the difference between an asset and a liability, and why spending more money on assets and less on liabilities leads to financial independence earlier in life. Countee Cullen once said: *"We must be one thing or the other, an asset or a liability, the sinew in your wing to help you soar, or the chain to bind you to earth."* I chose to be an asset, to not just my family but to the society at large. For this reason, I endeavour to practice doing what I learned, and I keep telling and helping others to do the same. It is my hope that you too are already an asset to Mother Earth, or on your way to becoming one.

I've always been fairly conservative when it comes to spending. But there have been occasions when my spending wasn't responsible. For instance, in 2003, we purchased a TriStar vacuum for $1600. That was insane! Why did I buy a vacuum that cost so much when I was living in a 3-bedroom townhome, and the first floor had no carpet? Because the salesperson was thorough and very convincing when he demonstrated how great the vacuum was. He instructed me to use my vacuum to clean a certain area, then he put a clean white filter in his vacuum and went over the same spot. Suffice to say he was correct; the evidence showed that my vacuum wasn't doing a great job. It was even more alarming when we did the drapes and mattresses.

What sold me, however, was when he shared that the vacuum had a lifetime warranty, and that I never had to purchase a vacuum again. In retrospect, I thought about how gullible I must have been. What does a lifetime warranty mean? But the truth is, I've never purchased another vacuum since, and it still performs very well. But despite my great experience with this vacuum, I still believe that was irresponsible spending. It took me two years to pay it off on an installment plan. I could have put that money towards my sons' university education, and the government would have matched the contribution with $320. I have other examples, although not as bizarre, but I shared this one to show that a lack of financial goals can cause you to make bad spending decisions, so the sooner you have a financial plan, the better your position.

I believe financial education is a lifelong learning journey, because I learn new things every week, sometimes every day. However, once I became more financially intelligent, my spending habits changed. I started using credit cards to make infinite returns, instead of using them to purchase unnecessary liabilities that took time to pay off. I also started to save and invest more. Later, when I realized that my investing efforts weren't generating the growth I desired, I started investing in real estate. By the fifth year into my real estate investing journey, I had acquired more than ten investment properties. At the time of writing this section, I still owned more than fifteen properties, and I had some more in new developments that would be closing later in the year, and the following year. This far exceeds my investment goals.

When I moved from my townhome, my objective was to own three more investment properties, bringing the total number of homes I owned to five, my principal home included. But after reading *Think and Grow Rich* and *The Science of Personal Achievement* by Napoleon Hill, *The Wealthy Barber* by David Chilton, and the *Rich Dad Poor Dad* series by Robert Kiyosaki, I had a shift in my paradigm. In my quest to learn even more about investing in real estate and achieving my definite purpose, I stumbled across the Karadza brothers, Nick and Tom Karadza at Rock Star Real Estate, and through them I met my real estate coach, John Paul Hunt. All their teachings, advice, and guidance allowed me to exceed my goal in a short period of time. And it didn't stop there; things got even better. Apart from my hands-on real estate investments, over the years I have also invested in land developments, storage facilities, and other real estate joint ventures that are hands-off. That is how powerful financial education is; it will help you to keep resetting your financial goals and achieving much more than you imagined

The Power of Negotiation

What is negotiation? When I typed this question into Google, I got a number of responses. After reading through some, I decided to use Investopedia's one. *"Negotiation is a strategic discussion that resolves an issue in a way that both parties find acceptable. In a negotiation, each party tries to persuade the other to agree with his or her point of view. By negotiating, all involved parties try to avoid arguing but agree to reach some form of compromise."*

When I was purchasing my first minivan, after I established the features I desired, I remember being very adamant about the payment I wanted to make monthly. While the salesperson was focused on the purchase price, the interest rate, and what the monthly payments would be, I kept on insisting on the amount I was willing to pay. I believe the conversation eventually got to an impasse because I stopped listening to what the salesperson had to say, and I suspected he had stopped listening to me as well. He thought the amount of monthly payments I shared was ridiculous, but he claimed he was going to talk to his manager and let me know the decision. He returned, beaming, and said that it was just as he thought: his manager confirmed exactly what he shared.

I was pregnant at the time and fully spent by then, so after listening to him, I got up and said: *"Very well then, I guess I won't be buying a minivan from you. Thank you for your time."* I saw the light leave his face as I extended my hand to bid him goodbye. Before I turned to get on my way, I heard: *"Wait, what if we can do something else for you?"* When I heard "something else," I assumed he meant a car instead of a van, so I immediately shared that if I wanted a car, I would have asked for one, and then I turned to leave. The salesperson hastened to share that I would get the minivan I wanted, but instead of a purchase, it would be a lease.

At the time, I wasn't familiar with leasing a vehicle because, in Jamaica, I was only aware of people buying their vehicles. After all the explanations and the back and forth, I ended up leasing the minivan and paying a bit less than what I wanted to. The minivan I ended up getting also had more features than what I'd stipulated, because the manager remembered that they had an Olympic Model Caravan that they wanted to sell, because the Olympics was over. Something that stood out for me, when the manager came out to shake my hand and to congratulate me, was when he said: "You're a great negotiator!"

Of course, I hadn't gone to the dealership expecting to negotiate. Moreover, negotiation wasn't even a part of my repertoire. I was relatively new in the country and trying to adapt. I was only certain about two things: 1) I wanted a minivan—not a car—because my in-laws were scheduled to visit around the time the baby would come, and I wanted everyone to fit in one vehicle, and 2) I was about to have another mouth to feed, a new mortgage, property taxes, and other new expenses, and my budget said I could only afford a certain payment. And for that reason, I stuck to my guns.

I later realized how powerful that negotiation strategy was—and of course, I'm only calling it "negotiation" because of the exchange with the manager at the dealership—and I have used it to purchase subsequent vehicles, homes, and furniture, and to bargain for mortgage interest rates, lines of credit interest rates, cable and internet payments, and much more. I have even used it to defer credit card payments at no interest charge to me.

Whenever I disclose some of the things I've negotiated over the years, with friends or co-workers, they sometimes look at me like I'm growing horns. But why? Because many of us are sheep. We take what people tell us at face value, and we don't question them. This is another area where school is failing many students. Despite the efforts being made in the education system to change this, for the most part, school doesn't cultivate a culture of questioning, and challenging the status quo, in students. In fact, when I was a student, there were times when I sensed a bit of resentment from a teacher, towards students who would ask "too many questions."

At the time, I too felt annoyed with those students. But I was a student myself, young and inexperienced, and some of my reactions were drawn from the teacher's. I later learned, however, that the questioning child (and I don't mean the child who asks silly questions to get some attention) is the one who does a lot of critical thinking, and therefore performs better in more noble situations. So, the next time you find yourself in a situation that goes against what you want to do or pay, prepare to negotiate. It could save you some money or earn you something more valuable than expected. Planning before taking action could be beneficial too, as you will know what works better for you, and you'll stick firmly to your decisions, and not easily swayed.

The Ability to Help Others

Audrey Hepburn once said: *"As you grow older, you will discover that you have two hands, one for helping yourself, the other for helping others."*

I strongly believe part of our mission here on Earth is to help others. If that wasn't the case, why would we feel so great when we render assistance to our neighbours. And neighbour, here, doesn't mean the person who lives next door; it's referring to every other person on planet Earth. It is such a wonderful feeling when you can inspire someone, provide some assistance to others to improve their situation, help someone to solve a problem, or even just help that person to acquire more knowledge.

I used to think that the rich and affluent don't like to share their wealth or knowledge with others. They only look out for their family members, and for those family members who seem to be in more need, even to a lesser extent. But as I read and listened to the stories of many affluent people over the years, I observed a common denominator among most of them. They love to help, and being in a financial position to help, gives them one of their greatest satisfactions. They also love to share their knowledge. They share their mistakes to safeguard others from making the same ones, they share their wealth with charity, they support medical researches, and they give back to the community in various forms. Some build schools, some fund community initiatives, some fund post-secondary education for the underprivileged, some fund women empowerment initiatives, and the list goes on.

Upon reflection, I realized my thinking was skewed. Over time, I gathered that some people speak out against the rich and affluent because they are looking for fish. They believe they are helped when someone gives them some fish. But the rich and affluent do not believe in giving out fish. They concur with what the wise ones say: *"Teach a person to fish instead of giving him fish. You give him fish, he may be able to eat for a day or two; you teach him how to fish, he can eat for the rest of his life."* I mentioned this before, but again think about a lottery player who suddenly has great riches, who ends up broke a few years later, or the child of a wealthy person who was given a large inheritance but blew it after a few years. This happens because they didn't know how to fish. Eventually, I learned that without the necessary skills to attain success, it doesn't matter how many fish you give to some people; they will ultimately become hungry again.

I've always been a cheerful giver, and I look for opportunities to contribute to a cause or to the wellbeing of others who are in need. Growing up in the church, I learned from an early age that God wants us to share with others, and that he blesses us whenever we do. With financial education, it became apparent that I could help on a larger scale if I have a strong financial foundation. Hence, I keep improving my financial position to be able to continue helping more. But I'm more mindful that although we should always aspire to help others, and that building a strong financial foundation provides the wherewithal to stretch a helping hand, I have to be cognizant of the type of assistance I'm providing. Teaching a person financial education is far more valuable than giving him a few thousand dollars.

The takeaway here is that we want people to be self-reliant; we don't want them to spend their lives depending on others. Therefore, helping others to acquire the necessary skills to build a strong financial foundation is a more significant help than doling out your wealth to them. So, I now focus more on helping people with financial education, so that they can improve their financial position to help themselves, their loved ones, and even share with others.

Peace of Mind

In 2002, when Richard got laid off, and I was supposed to be on maternity leave, life looked dim. Before I go on, let me share a huge misconception about maternity leave in Canada, which I suspect that most people didn't realize until reality kicked in. It's great that Canada allows parents to take a full year maternity or paternity leave without your job being in jeopardy, but as great as that may sound, there can be a downside to this opportunity, depending on your income level and employer.

Some employers will top up your employment insurance income while you're on maternity leave. But if your employer is like mine, who doesn't top up, the income you receive during maternity leave could be greatly reduced from your regular one.

Let's get back on track as to why this section is titled "Peace of Mind." In 2002, when Richard got laid off after I decided to shorten my maternity leave, I got worried. I had cut my maternity leave short because of the post 911 effect on the economy, and his workplace was doing a lot of restructuring and had laid off some employees. The thought of us living on two unemployment incomes was very scary, so I didn't want to take the chance, and I was absolutely glad that I had gone back to work early. Even though my income wasn't sufficient to cover the mortgage, make two car payments, insurance payments, cover household expenses, and contribute to my elder son's education savings plan, and Richard's retirement savings plan, I found a way to make things work.

That was only two years after arriving in Canada, and it was the same year we purchased our townhome and leased a minivan. For that reason, most of our savings were depleted from mortgage down payment, closing costs, buying additional furniture, and much more. And did I mention that my younger son was born on Mother's Day, the same year? Oh, yes! The year 2002 will go down as my most eventful year, for a number of reasons. It was the year I:

1. Became a family of four
2. Experienced the true meaning of Mother's Day
3. Learned that babies could be used as a timer
4. Closed on my first home in Canada
5. Leased a vehicle for the first time
6. Got my master's in juggling credit cards to avoid paying interest
7. Got my PhD in stretching my income
8. Learned that God can sustain me on 3 or 4 hours of sleep each night (I had a 4-month-old son, was moved to a new school, and was teaching three new courses.)
9. Learned that God will carry me when I have no energy to move myself
10. Realized that I had to put myself in a better financial position so that, should another year like 2002 come, I would have peace of mind instead of worrying that I may have to return my leased minivan

Earlier, I shared that when I was growing up, my grandfather always reminded me that it was important to have something put away for a rainy day. And although it sounds clichéd, that saying has served me very well to this day. Had my grandfather's saying not rang true to me, perhaps I would have purchased the minivan at the time. After I listened to the pros and cons of leasing and financing, I had opted for leasing, since it meant I could hold on to some of my savings. And my goodness, how glad I was that I did that. The out-of-pocket was much less for leasing compared to financing, and I wanted an affordable monthly payment.

That savings helped to keep me and my family afloat until Richard started receiving unemployment insurance, more than a month after his employment was terminated. Our combined income still wasn't enough to cover all the expenses, but the extra income certainly helped. I never missed a mortgage payment, a car payment, or any financial obligations for that matter. We couldn't do dinner and a movie once or twice a month like we usually did; and on Fridays, we had home-prepared meals instead of takeout. But the sacrifices taught me very useful lessons: I learned to live on a strict budget, to stretch our income, and to juggle credit cards so that I could get the longest time to pay. It was then that I recognized that credit cards were a great invention, and a tool that could be used to save money. During that time, I accumulated zero consumer debt, and I never paid a dime for interest.

The lessons I learned that year helped me to have peace of mind today— peace of mind knowing that the loss of a job will not cause me to run scared again. I have put myself in a position to weather the storm, by increasing my financial IQ and embarking on investment ventures that make me far better off than I was in 2002. I learned that less can be more— having less money doesn't have to lead to bad debt or bankruptcy. But ultimately, I know with confidence that despite how bleak the situation appears, with God's help, all will be just fine.

These are the skills that students need to learn, and the stories that they need to hear. Financial education will help you to weather the financial storm and make you better for it. But if you lack the knowledge to conduct your financial affairs effectively, and make informed decisions about money, and you have a year like my 2002, for instance, you may fair differently. Financial education is paramount; even in small doses, it will help to give you peace of mind.

Living Life on My Terms

It is very difficult to live life on your own terms if you don't have a strong financial footing or a nest egg, so to speak. If you don't invest in yourself for the future, you will feel like you're moving from job to job, with no real goal or purpose but to earn some money to cover your expenses. Or you may have had the same position for the past 10 or 20 years, but nothing has really changed. Some people will say you need to write down your goals regularly so that you can read them daily and keep working towards them. And that may work very well for most people—there was a time when I would write down my goals regularly—but my problem is that I can never stick to that ritual. I may be gung-ho for some days, maybe even weeks, about writing and reading my goals regularly, but I never last for even six months, never mind a year.

Hence, I eventually gave up and conceded that that doesn't work well for me. But what appears to work is the power of autosuggestion and the law of attraction. If you have read Napoleon Hill's book, *Think and Grow Rich*, you should be familiar with the term *autosuggestion*. And if you watched *The Secret*, with Bob Proctor and Jack Canfield, you should know about the law of attraction. I regularly think about my goals, mull them over in my head, talk to God about them, imagine myself achieving them, and take action to realize them. That seems to work better for me. So, although from time to time I still try to write them down and read them, I mostly stick to the methods I mentioned above.

I do still need a lot of work with the law of attraction and the power of autosuggestion though, because I sometimes allow that little voice in my head to limit my desire to soar. At times, that little voice causes me to listen to people and care more about what they say than what I'm convinced is smarter thinking. I had the opportunity to meet Bob Proctor and Jack Canfield, and I listened to them speak. I was in awe, especially of Bob Proctor and how much he believes in the law of attraction, and how much he lives his life believing he can achieve whatever he puts his mind to.

It's something I continue to work on, but sometimes I feel that the limitations I place on myself are a manifestation of how I was grown. My grandparents were Christians, so naturally I grew up with Christian principles, and I eventually became a Christian when I was a teenager. While I was always raised to reach for the stars, somehow there was an undertone in the church that it didn't apply to financial success. I always felt that Christians should be modest when it comes to wanting to earn more money, especially when the topic of the sermon was: *"The love of money is the root of all evil."* There were also times when I felt like my grandmother, especially, made a concerted effort to give a lot to the church and the community, so they would inevitably end up with less.

While I believe in sharing with others, when I was growing up, I used to think my grandparents would have much more for themselves and our family if they gave less to people who I sometimes didn't even know. But I would always remember that the bible talked about how difficult it is for a rich man to enter the kingdom of God. The scripture says that it's easier for a camel to go through the eye of a needle than for a rich person to enter the kingdom of God. As I intend to be in God's kingdom one day, that saying still affects me from time to time.

I do, however, believe that you can help more when you have more. For instance, the more knowledge I have about finances, the more I can share with you; the more money I have, the more I can help my family members and others financially. So, it's actually a bit mind-boggling since the scriptures also talk about the importance of giving. I know giving doesn't have to be about money. But let's face it; everyone needs money to live, and the less money you have, the less quality of life you'll enjoy. A lack of money is what causes some people to accumulate bad debt, and what causes countries around the world to be facing a debt crisis. So, doesn't it make better sense that we should all learn the skills to make more money? Which means that reaching for the sky, where money is concerned, should be at the top of everybody's list of goals.

I still have ways to go; I'm not fully there yet, but my goal is to live life on my own terms through and through, and I do wish the same for you as well. My terms may be very different from yours, but it doesn't matter; as long as you feel in control of your life and where you're heading, your life's journey will be more fulfilling and satisfying. The key is to acquire a high level of financial intelligence, and build a strong financial foundation. This will improve our lifestyle and well-being, and that of our family and loved ones too. So, when we are financially secured, we are definitely more empowered to live life on our own terms, and that is part of my definite purpose.

Leaving a Legacy

I believe everyone would like to leave a legacy behind after their time on this Earth expires. I know I do. What about you—do you want to leave a legacy?

People want to be remembered for something they contributed to their loved ones, their community, or to the world at large. This legacy can take various forms. Some people want to leave funds for their children and grandchildren so that they can have a better life, or funds for a charity in order to help people with basic needs, or to start a foundation to advance a medical research, or for church ministries, and the list goes on.

I've been teaching for the past 23 years, so part of my legacy, or my contributions that I hope have impacted and will continue to impact the world on a large scale, is my teaching. Some of my students became parents, social workers, engineers, dentists, doctors, computer scientists, accountants, mechanics, and more. I believe they are making their mark. My new mission to spread the importance of financial literacy, and share why it is important to teach financial education in school, is another way that I'll be leaving my footprint. To support my mission, I will be starting a financial literacy club at my school, for the 2019-2020 school year. There, I will work with students to focus on:

- Spending/buying and saving wisely
- Using credit cards wisely; capitalizing on the rewards benefits
- Saving for emergency funds
- Leasing vs financing a car
- Buying vs renting a home
- Credit scores: importance and impact
- Investing for retirement
- Investing for children's education: impact of student loan
- Assets vs liabilities: good debt vs bad debt
- Insurance protection: how it protects families in unexpected crises
- Investing in real estate vs mutual funds/stocks and bonds

Despite my teaching legacy, whether inside or outside the classroom, I wouldn't be able to say that I've found my truth if I wasn't able to leave a monetary legacy for my children, grandchildren, my favourite charity, and my church. I believe that financial education has helped me to journey down my truthful path. If I didn't acquire a high level of financial intelligence, I would still be searching for my truth. Whether you want to leave a monetary legacy or not, if you don't believe you have a high level of financial intelligence, it is time to start investing your time, effort, and more, to increase your financial IQ. This will put you in a much better position to leave the legacy or the lasting footprint that you want the lives you touch to remember. So, join me in the next chapter, where you will learn about the role you can play in helping to relieve the debt crisis in our countries, by leaving large footprints of financial education for your family and subsequent generations.

10
The Debt Crisis Consumers Face

"I think we are not serious about attacking the long-term debt problem, and that's one of the things that he's going to have to find a way to get on the agenda."

—Michael Bloomberg

What Is Government Doing?

The governments of Canada and the United States indeed recognize the need for financial literacy among its residence because, in 2004, the US Senate passed a resolution to officially recognize April as Financial Literacy Month, and in 2005, the House of Representatives passed a bill supporting the Senate's resolution. This move was to help Americans improve their understanding about financial matters such as saving, debt, credit management, and purchasing a home. Eight years later, the Financial Consumer Agency of Canada (FCAC) dubbed November as Canada's Financial Literacy Month. My research shows that the FCAC has an online Canadian Financial Literacy Database, with resources aimed at creating awareness about financial education for Canadians. The database provides links to resources such as personal finance calculators or tools, financial education programs, videos, books, articles, workshops, worksheets, games, events, available funding programs, etc. However, the million-dollar question is: How many Americans and Canadians are aware of these initiatives?

For instance, if you're a Canadian resident, ask yourself these questions. Did you know that November is Financial Literacy Month? Have you ever heard about the FCAC? The only reason I became aware of the FCAC was because the topic I did for my master's capstone was the importance of financial literacy, and the impact it has on adults' lifestyle and well-being. Hence, I just happened to stumble across this during my research to complete my paper. You would think something that is so important wouldn't be the best kept secret. The Canadian Government should have been paying for TV commercials to share this with the public, and to explain to the masses why financial education is essential. Governments don't hesitate to pay for commercials to take cheap shots at the opposition, so why can't they invest in commercials to lead their citizens to financial educational resources? And that is just one mode that can be used to effect change.

There's a myriad of strategies that governments can use to spread the importance of financial education to help people to improve their finances and stay out of debt. It is still very disappointing that with the looming consumer debt crisis, governments still don't see the need to alter the school curriculum to include even a mandatory financial literacy course that covers the basic skills that young people need to conduct their financial affairs. Every high school graduate should leave school with knowledge of at least basic personal finance. They should know how to make money and save effectively. They should learn to pay themselves first. They should know the difference between an asset and a liability. They should learn the importance of credit scores and how to maintain great scores, and how to file their income taxes, buy a home, and save for their retirement and their children's education. We are not teaching our children to be financially successful in life. And this is not only affecting individual families; it's also affecting the economy at large.

When I was in elementary school in Jamaica, every Tuesday was designated as banking day. My grandmother or grandfather would give me two or five dollars to bank. One of my teachers would collect the money and write the amount I deposited on my bank card. When all the entries on the card were filled out, I got a red bank book. From time to time, my grandmother would bring my book to the bank for it to be updated to reflect accrued interest. If my memory serves me right, the government partnered with the Workers Bank of Jamaica, at the time, to execute this.

It was a very small gesture, but the lessons taught from this were multifold. Apart from the obvious one, the importance of saving, I learned the following things as well:

1. **Responsibility**: It was my responsibility to remind my grandparents about banking day and to take my money to school.
2. **Consistent Saving**: I wanted to receive the red bank book, and that meant I had to fill up my bank card first. It didn't matter if I missed a week and brought more money to bank the following week. Only one entry was done for any given week.
3. **Patience**: I can't remember how many entries were on the card, but it sure felt like it took forever to fill up.
4. **Accomplishment and Ownership**: Each week when I saw my total increase, I felt a sense of pride and accomplishment. Whenever I received additional pocket money from loved ones, instead of running to buy candies—not that I had to because my grandparents had a small grocery store—I saved it for banking day.

Saving two or five dollars per week may sound like nothing, but let me share a story about that red bank book. When I went to high school, the school savings program wasn't offered anymore, so I stopped using the red bank book. My grandmother died shortly after, and I went to live with my mom in Kingston, Jamaica. I got another bank card, but it was with a different bank in Kingston. When I was completing high school, my grandfather fell ill, and my mom (an only child) gave up her small business venture to go back to my childhood community to care for him. Some months after, my mom stumbled upon my red bank book. We had no idea what my total balance was because my book hadn't been updated for about 8 years. As my mom wasn't working at the time, and the expenses were increasing, her savings were depleting.

Eventually, she had to seek employment. But prior to her getting a job, the expenses started to overwhelm her and, on one occasion, she shared that she really needed some financial assistance.

Since I was attending university, working only on summer holidays and semester breaks, my older brother, who had a full-time job, was her primary source of help. I was a great saver, however, thanks to the lessons I'd learned from elementary school; and from time to time, I would help my mom with the expenses for my grandfather. One day, my mom called to say that she needed some supplies for my grandfather, but she was running very low on cash. During the discussion, I remembered my red bank book. As her name was already on my account, since one parent's name was required, I told her to take the book to the bank and withdraw the funds to buy the supplies. After the interest was applied, she ended up with close to $800, which was over and beyond what she needed to get the supplies. And if you're a Jamaican and thinking that $800 is not a lot of money, in 1992, $800 would have perhaps fetched you what $10,000 would get you today in 2019.

Your Children Will Carry the Burden

The debt crises in many first world countries is causing a strain on the world's economy. If we as a people don't do something now to stop the high consumer debt in our countries, our children will pay a high price. In Canada, reports show that by the end of 2018, Canadians owed $1.78 for every dollar of income they earned. This represents an 8.5% increase since 2014, when that amount was $1.64. Consumer debt in the United States, by the end of 2018, was $13.3 trillion. At the end of 2015, consumer debt was $11.8 trillion. This means, in three years, the debt in the US rose $1.5 trillion, which represents a 12.7% increase in consumer debt. As salaries are not moving to keep up with inflation, many households will start relying on credit to help supplement their expenses.

Although not all consumer debt is considered bad, whether good or bad, debt in general affects a country's economy. Consumer debt includes:

- Home loans
- Student loans
- Auto loans
- Personal loans
- Bank credit cards
- Retail credit cards

Loans that are tied to assets—a rental home mortgage for instance—aren't the loans that are concerning. The loans that are taken for consumables are the ones that we need to pay closer attention to. Despite the type of loan you have, however, there are different strategies you can use to reduce your debt, which I'll discuss next.

Debt Consolidation

If you have debt in multiple places, if possible, take out one big loan that will cover all your debt. Doing this will cause you to be able to track your debt better, and you will have a single monthly debt payment. If you have one loan payment, the likelihood of you forgetting to make a payment is very slim.

Choose loans that have lower interest rates, because your monthly payments will be stretched further. For instance, if you have credit card loans, it will be cheaper to apply for a secured or unsecured line of credit. A secured line of credit, usually a HELOC (explained in an earlier chapter), has an interest rate as low as the prime lending rate, which at the time of writing this section is 3.95% in Canada, and 5.5% in the United States. An unsecured LOC usually has a higher rate than a HELOC, but certainly not as high as the 20% or more that many credit card companies charge.

A term loan also has lower interest rates than a credit card loan. And term loans help you to pay off your loan faster since the loan is amortized over a specified term—5 years for example. And unlike a LOC that has the interest-only payment option (which may tempt some people to make only the minimum payment), with term loans, your monthly payments include interest and principal. This alternative will help you to pay off your balance much faster.

Pay More Frequently

The bills for loans are usually generated monthly, and the bill due date is normally disclosed. For this reason, most people pay their bills once per month. However, if you're paid weekly or biweekly, making a payment each time you get paid will reduce your loan faster, and this will also reduce the amount of interest you pay overall. For example, if you pay your mortgage biweekly instead of monthly, your 25-year mortgage could be paid off in 20 years or less. This will save you at least five years' worth of interest.

Make Lump Sum Payments

Most mortgages have a lump sum payment option that allows you to pay a percentage of your outstanding balance at one time. Capitalizing on this when you come into some money, such as tax refunds, an inheritance, and bonuses, will not only reduce your mortgage faster, it can significantly decrease the amount of interest paid. Lump-sum payments are applied directly to the principal; thus, your outstanding balance is reduced immediately. A lower principal results in lower interest charges, which eventually leads to considerable savings.

Pay Off Debts With Shorter Time First

Not everyone is able to get a debt consolidation loan, and you may be asking: What if I can't get one loan to cover all my debt; what do I do? Another strategy you can use is to pay off the debt that has the shortest time in which it will be paid off. For instance, suppose you have two debts you're trying to pay off. For the purpose of explanation, I will call one debt A, and the other debt B. If debt A will be paid off earlier than debt B, based on your current payment plan, make only the minimum payment on debt B, and put everything else toward paying off debt A. Once debt A is paid off, put all the payments toward debt B. And if you find that you can put some extra toward paying off the debts even faster, commit to doing that.

Everyone who has consumer debt, especially, should be using strategies like these to get out of debt faster. And once the debts are all paid off, they should save the amount they were using to service their debts, invest it into something profitable, and vow never to get back into bad debt again. If everyone practices doing this, over the next decade or two, consumer debt will be reduced considerably, and our children will not be saddled with the heavy debt burden in the future.

Tracking Your Expenses Helps

Were you ever in the checkout line when the cashier announced the embarrassing news that your card was declined? I have heard that punch line a few times, but certainly not for the reason you're thinking, so wipe that smirk off your face right now. My card was never declined because of overspending. In fact, I've never managed to make enough purchases to max out any of my credit cards. The most popular reason for my card declining was almost always card expiration. And this is because I don't listen to Richard when he tells me to stop using the old card and activate the new one that comes in the mail. A less common reason is when the bank shuts down my card because they suspect fraudulent activities. Although both situations are annoying and sometimes unavoidable, it is a great feeling knowing that I've never had to wonder if there was enough on my credit card to cover my purchases.

One of the reasons many consumers overspend is because they do not track their expenses. If you're using only debit cards to make purchases, this may become noticeable when you're at the checkout line and the cashier announces the dreaded news: *"Your card is declined."* At that moment, it becomes apparent that you have no funds in your account to pay for your purchases. On the other hand, if you use credit cards to pay for almost everything like I do, and your cards are maxed, you may be able to use your debit card, assuming you have money in your bank account to pay. But if all your cards are declined, you're in deep, deep, you know what, because that would mean your credit cards are maxed, you're in debt, and you have no money to pay for your purchases.

Tracking your expenses and account balances will prevent embarrassing situations like these, as you will always be aware of your expenditures and how much money you have to go around. The big mistake some consumers make is believing that their credit card is an extension to their bank account. Hence, they spend the money in their checking account and still use the credit card, knowing very well there's no money left in their account to pay off the balance. Consequently, they make only the minimum payment monthly, which puts them into deeper debt each month, and credit card debt is the worst debt to have. There are hidden charges that never seem to be traceable. Here is a list of some simple ideas that you can use to track your expenses:

1. Create a budget and stick to it. Budgets were discussed in a previous chapter, so I don't need to expand any more on this.

2. Record your expenses in each category in your budget, and adjust your income balance each time. Some expenses such as rent, mortgages, insurance, and car payments are fixed every month, so those should be entered first. The variable expenses, such as groceries, transportation, and entertainment, are the ones that really need tracking.

3. Stay on top of your variable expenses. If you find that one month you're overspending in one category, and it's unavoidable, you may want to cut back in another category so that you're still staying within your budget.

A budget not only helps you to track your income and expenditures; it also helps you to see where the bulk of your money is going each month. Frequently, the savings category is the one that gets hit first when your budget is out of whack. But if you pay yourself first, like I shared before, the savings category should be treated as a fixed cost, so that from the onset, you know how much you have to spend each month. In the event of a big unexpected expense, your savings can come in handy.

I don't recommend you use all your savings for big expenses, however. Always try to see where you can cut back for a few months to cover those expenses first. Using your credit card can be helpful too, because you get that grace period before you have to pay your balance. And do remember the example I shared, in the credit card section, which affords you the maximum time to pay for your purchases without having to pay an interest penalty.

Buying Smart Helps

Shopping for Food Items

I'm not a fan of cutting out coupons, and to be honest, I sometimes get impatient when the person ahead of me in the cash-out line has a bunch of coupons that the cashier has to read to ensure they are usable. With the advance in technology, I think suppliers can do a much better job of helping consumers to save a few bucks (a few stores like Costco seem to have this covered). But for those who are okay with cutting out coupons, this is certainly a way to save on purchases. There is also a bunch of flyers that come each week in your local paper, with the items on discount and the pertinent stores.

If you're like me and don't like flipping through papers, I have an app on my smartphone, called Flipp, which allows me to click on the store where I'll be shopping, and it shows a list of items that are discounted, and the time frame. You can compare prices at different stores too, and see where you can get the cheapest buy, and even ask for a price match. One of the cashiers at my main grocery store told me about it more than 2 years ago, but I've honestly used it only once—about the same time I installed it. I remembered about it when I was writing this paragraph, so I accessed it on my phone in an effort to share how it really works.

What I discovered during the process was that you can actually click on the items of interest and it populates your shopping list. And if you click on items from multiple stores, the items in your shopping list are compartmentalized under each store. I believe this is a more effective way to save time and money. The shopping list shows the items you need so that you can pick up only the things you really need, and not indulge in spontaneous buying. Of course, that is providing you're not like Richard, who goes shopping and comes back with a bunch of things not on the list, while the main item I asked him to purchase is missing.

What about other purchases?

Before making a purchase, especially an expensive one, it's always wise to do some homework first. Identify what you plan to buy, and determine if it's a need or something you just want to have. If it's just a nice-to-have, and not a necessity, perhaps you should reconsider making that purchase. If it's a need, however, decide on how much you can afford to spend, and then research the product, prices, and suppliers. Compare prices among suppliers, and since quality is key, it's prudent to read reviews on the product, and on the return policies of the suppliers. As some online reviews may not be useful, it's good practice to ask people you know for recommendations.

Buying goods and services on sale or off-season can be very beneficial. For example, a lot of the décor I use to decorate my home and tree for Christmas, were purchased after Christmas, at 50% to 70% off the regular prices. And I have—in the words of friends and colleagues—a magazine perfect Christmas tree. Most of my clothes, jewellery, and accessories were purchased at reduced prices as well. And by reduced prices, I don't necessarily mean clearance. Many department stores like The Bay, Macy's, and JC Penny offer regular family and friends discounted days that I capitalize on. Thus, on some occasions, I save up to 50% on purchases during these times.

Some higher-end stores also offer huge discounts at the outlet malls or during certain seasons. Two of my favourite stores, Victoria's Secret and Bath and Body Works, have two semi-annual sales each year, and the deals offer great saving opportunities. Some stores offer significant reductions on items from the previous year, even when the items look exactly the same as those in the current year. This is similar to how a car dealership sells a 2018 model of a car, cheaper than the 2019 model, even though both models are identical.

The takeaway here is that you should budget, do your research, plan your spending, and look for deals before you part with your money. Saving a few bucks here and there can lead to significant savings that you didn't anticipate. And every dollar you save can be put toward your investments or paying down your debt.

Avoid Consumer Debt

Buy What Is Needed

Avoid buying nice-to-haves unless you have enough cash to cover such purchases. If you're using credit cards to purchase things you don't need and cannot afford, that is a sure way to get you into debt very fast.

Emergency Funds

Pay yourself 10 to 15% first, from each paycheck, and set aside a portion of that 15% for emergency funds. Your emergency funds should be 3 to 6 months' worth of income. Even if you use credit cards to pay for emergency repairs, you can pay off your balance using the emergency funds you saved. And if it's not sufficient to cover everything, you still have other monies that you can borrow from, because you were in the habit of saving.

Having an emergency fund is a great way to avoid bad debt. Life is filled with many surprise expenses and, in many cases, they occur at a time when you least expect them. Not having an emergency fund often forces you to borrow money when something unexpected comes up. Most people borrow money from their lines of credit—if they have one—or they use the most popular way to get access to cash fast: their credit cards. But this is not a wise practice, and should be an exception to the rule.

Be Smart With Credit Cards

While credit cards are very useful to help with emergency funds, because you get a grace period, misusing them is one of the fastest ways to get into bad debt. Many people get into credit card debt because they are ignorant about how they really work. Sometimes the reason for the initial debt is justified. For instance, an unexpected car or house repair expense. You use your credit card to pay for the repairs, with good intentions to pay off the balance as soon as possible. However, the notion of a minimum payment tempted you. You tell yourself that this time you'll just pay one half the balance—after all, you are only required to make the minimum payment—but the next time, you'll pay the bill in full. You didn't realize that once your balance is not paid in full, interest is charged on all subsequent purchases.

Therefore, your next bill has a much higher balance than you anticipated (due to unexplained interest charges), and you're unable to pay your balance in full. Sometimes another unexpected expense comes up that causes you to put a more substantial amount on the card, which is to your chagrin considering you hadn't paid off the previous balance. Hence, the Ferris wheel of high-interest charges begins, and you can never seem to jump off. Sooner or later, you're not paying even half your bill anymore; you're paying just the minimum payment, and you become fully hooked. Don't pay only the minimum payment; pay the full balance on your credit card each month. If you can't pay off the balance in full, that's a sign that you're spending more than you can afford. So, cut back on your spending, and try to avoid charging your card until your balance is zero.

Cash Advances and Balance Transfers

Avoid cash advances on your credit cards because interest starts to accrue the moment you take them. As explained earlier, there is no grace period with cash advances. You should also avoid doing balance transfers from one credit card to another if there's no promotional interest rate or zero percent balance transfer fee. For existing cards, there's usually a balance transfer fee involved that increases your debt, so read the fine print. And if you have a balance transfer promotional rate, try to pay off the card by the time the promotion expires, because at the end of the promotion, interest will start to accrue daily on your outstanding balance.

Limit Your Exposure

If you know you're not a disciplined spender, limit the number of credit cards you have, and ask your credit card company to restrict your credit limit. A higher limit means you have the potential to spend more than you can afford, thus putting yourself in more debt. Also, using more cards makes it more challenging to track balances and be on top of your payments. My suggestion is to keep a card for unexpected large expenses. This way, if you need time to pay off emergency expenses, only that amount will be charged interest, and not all your purchases. You will still have the grace period on your other card, for your regular purchases.

Be Smart With Lines of Credit

A line of credit (LOC) has a much lower interest rate than a credit card, and the interest is calculated according to simple interest, unlike a credit card where interest is calculated according to compound interest. Simple interest is a cheaper way to pay interest because interest is charged only on the principal amount borrowed. Compound interest, on the other hand, is more expensive because interest is calculated on previous interest charged. For this reason, you may opt to use your LOC for a purchase before first thinking through things. But sometimes, depending on how long you need to borrow the money, it may be wiser to use a credit card to capitalize on the grace period instead of having to pay interest from day one. Let's look at two examples involving a LOC and a credit card.

Line of Credit Example

Suppose you borrowed $10,000 on your LOC, at 5% per year, to make a purchase. Your daily interest rate is 0.05 divided by 365.

Hence, your daily interest charge, until your bill is generated, is $1.37 (10,000 x 0.05/365). If each month, you pay just your minimum balance, and your loan amount is unchanged, then every day of the year, your charge is $1.67.

Credit Card Example

Suppose you made a purchase of $10,000 on your credit card, at 15% per year. Your daily interest rate is 0.15 divided by 365.

For simplicity, lets assume you haven't been paying off your credit card balance in full. If your credit card company charges interest based on the average daily balance, on day one of the month, your interest charge will be $4.1096 (10,000 x 0.15/365).

On day two of the month, your interest charge will be $4.111 (10,004.1096 x 0.15/365).

On day three of the month, your interest charge will be $4.113 (10,008.2206 x 0.15/365).

From the examples, it looks like the LOC is better, but that depends, because if you know you'll be able to pay off the balance by the time your credit card bill is generated, it is better to use your credit card instead of your LOC for the purchase. Since there is no grace period with LOCs, interest starts to accrue the day you borrow the funds. And even if you know you won't be able to pay off your credit card bill in full, it's still better to use your credit card to make the purchase, to capitalize on the no-interest grace period and the potential reward points. And when the bill is due, that's the time you use your LOC to pay off your credit card if you're unable to pay off the remaining balance.

If it's funds that you need and not a purchase to make, I recommend you use your LOC. If you take cash advances on your credit card, there is no interest-free grace period. You will be charged interest compounded daily on the amount taken immediately. And since your credit card has a higher interest rate than your LOC, it's better to take the funds from your LOC, especially since it charges simple interest.

However, like credit cards, LOCs have a minimum payment that is just the interest payment. So even if you cannot afford to pay off your balance in full, try to pay as much as you can each month. Moreover, if you are paid multiple times in a month, try to make some payments as soon as you're paid, because interest is calculated daily, and the faster you reduce your balance, the less interest you will pay.

Start Your Financial Literacy Journey

It is not too late to embark on a journey to increase your financial intelligence. There are many books, YouTube videos, podcasts, seminars, webinars, and other online resources that you can access to help you as you journey to become financially literate. For example, *The Science of Money* by Brian Tracy and *The Wealthy Barber* by David Chilton are books about financial education that is easy to understand, and that you can read through quickly. Robert Kiyosaki, a huge proponent of the importance of having a high financial IQ, has written various books that will help you to start shifting your thinking when it comes to investing and managing your finances. He also has many YouTube videos and podcasts that you can access at the click of some keys, which will help to educate you financially. And there are many other authors and podcasters like Robert, whose missions are to help you to increase your financial IQ.

There are also free financial education programs that you can access online that will result in a deep structural shift in the way you think and feel, and in the actions you take, regarding matters relating to your money. These programs will help you to transform your financial practices and improve your financial health and well-being. For instance, during my research, I came across two free online financial education programs, *Money Smart* and *Smart About Money*. The *Smart About Money* program says it is dedicated to inspiring empowered financial decision making for individuals and families through every stage of life. And it offers free online self-directed programs that provide articles, resources, tools such as calculators and online budgeting, and tips to reinforce money management through life's ups and downs.

The *Smart About Money* program also has a website that is like a blog. It is called *On Your Own*, where you can find tips, articles, resources, and tools to help you understand financial basics, and make decisions based on your life situation. There, everyone is encouraged to share their own stories about credit, debt, money management, saving and investing, and other financially related attributes. You can email questions or interview people who are knowledgeable in finances, like financial planners, and experts on various money-related topics. It also provides questions that you should be asking, and information to look out for as you navigate your personal finances.

Blogs like these will help you recognize that you're not alone in your financial struggles and money challenges. It will also force you to acknowledge the truths about the financial world you have been thrown into, and to identify the lessons on finances you were not taught in school, so that you can now teach your children those lessons, so they don't fall victim to the system. You will also be able to learn from others' mistakes and emulate useful practices that can prevent you from making financial pitfalls, or that may help you to solve financial problems and even change your world views about money and planning for the future.

Besides reading books and engaging in financial education programs, even your smartphone is very useful in helping you to improve your finances. Various smartphone applications are available to help you with budgeting, tracking your credit scores, and money management. For example, *Mint*, a money management service, will send you alerts when your bills are due and when your account balance is low. Another app, *Personal Capital*, can be used to track investments, access research, and view other financial information online. And if you're thinking about automatic saving options, like saving for your children's education or your retirement, you can use *SavedPlus* to automatically transfer a pre-set amount of money from your checking account to your savings account.

Although school didn't teach you financial education, you are lucky to be living in this era where information can be easily accessed on the internet, and our smartphones have multiple apps that we can use to help manage our finances. I was at a seminar once, when the keynote speaker said, *"You don't know what you don't know until you know."* At first, I was rather puzzled by the statement, and I wondered what the point was of saying it. But after repeating it a few times, it became apparent what he meant. Having read this book, you can no longer say that no one taught you the importance of financial education and why you should become financially literate. At the end of the book, there is a page with a recommended reading list and recommended websites. There you will find several great books and resources on financial education. So start your financial education journey today; even small doses of financial literacy will help you to improve your lifestyle and the lifestyle of your family members.

Now that I have shared about the devastating impact that the lack of financial education among consumers has on the debt crisis in our country, continue reading to understand how you can make a difference in changing the trajectory of your life, and the experiences of your loved ones. I will also share how the destructive cycle of bad debt and bankruptcy can be thwarted if even small doses of financial education is included in the school curriculum, since this would help consumers to be more selective and strategic with matters surrounding their finances.

11
It's Time for Change

"My parents believed in education and economic security, and I thank them for it. Because I think that's part of what's made my life stable. It was instilled in me. You have to be able to pay your bills. You do not get into debt. And I never have been."

—Helen Mirren

Who Is Giving You Financial Advice?

Many people with poor financial literacy skills tend to seek out a financial advisor to help them with their financial planning or investment ventures. I have sat down with multiple financial advisors over the years to listen to their advice, and to glean what I could from the meetings. And what I've observed over time is that some financial advisors need financial advice themselves. Many of them promote only mutual funds and dollar-cost averaging, which is not my preferred way to invest since it feels somewhat like gambling. They also preach that you should diversify your portfolio, and yet their chant is about why you should buy this mutual fund or that one, and which funds are considered prudent, moderate, or risky in their performances.

But how can a portfolio that has mutual funds only be considered diversified? Is it the portfolio that is diversified, or is it the type of risks that are involved? Shouldn't a diversified portfolio consist of various asset classes? Advisor's explanations about diversification have always been mind-boggling for me. You cannot take financial advice from people who are inexperienced in that area. As George Clason, author of *The Richest Man in Babylon*, said: *"Advice is one thing that is freely given away, but watch that you take only what is worth having. He who takes advice about his savings from one who is inexperienced in such matters, shall pay with his savings for proving the falsity of their opinions."*

Very few financial advisors own other asset classes like a small business or real estate investments, and these are the only few who will advise that having a side business or real estate in your portfolio is a great idea. And you may be saying, "I don't want to own real estate because I don't want to clean toilets," as I've heard some people said, but do you think Robert Kiyosaki and Grant Cardone, who earn millions in real estate investments, clean bathrooms?

In fact, what is so daunting or wrong with cleaning bathrooms? Henry Ford said, *"Nothing is particularly hard if you divide it into small jobs."*

When we first started our real estate journey, and we closed on a single-family home, cleaning up the home and getting it ready for our tenants was like a family outing. Richard, the boys and their grandma, and I would load up into the minivan, and off we would go to get the home in tip-top shape. Even my girlfriend came to help a few times. By the time we were done, the house would look and smell so great that we got emotionally attached and wanted to stay. In fact, it felt no different from when we bought our primary home—a resale home—and family members chipped in to clean and deodorize it before we moved in.

As we increased our property holdings, hiring cleaners made much more sense, especially when an impromptu family outing wasn't possible because the properties are in cities far from home. But on occasion, when I visit some properties before new tenants move in, I am sometimes dissatisfied with the cleaning job and the freshness of the home. For this reason, sometimes I still travel with some scented candles and plug-in air fresheners, to leave in the homes in an effort to create the sweet freshness I like, and to give the home my personal touch.

Every successful investment and business venture has a starting point and a goal bar. The height of the bar should keep increasing over time. If you imagine yourself starting a business, and you see yourself doing the same thing five years later, that is not a business you expect to be growing, so do reconsider your thinking. When it comes to investments and business ventures, you must do your own research and seek the advice of those who achieved great success in that field. As Jim Rohn said, *"Formal education will make you a living. Self-*

education will make you a fortune." No one is more interested in your financial success than you, so invest in educating yourself, and be very selective about the people you take advice from.

Focus on What's Applicable

The time value of money (TVM) is a concept that everyone should learn. The TVM concept says a sum of money today is worth more than that same sum of money next week. Why? Because of the power of investing and compound interest. Money has the potential to grow over a period of time because it earns interest. So, if you need a sum of money in the future, you can invest less today at a specified interest rate and compounding period, to realize that amount in the future. For instance, the *Rule of 72* states that if you want to know how long it will take your investment to double at a fixed interest rate, you should just divide 72 by the interest rate. So, let's say you want your money to double in 8 years, the investment strategy you choose should yield a 9% return annually.

Let's look at the next two examples to get some understanding of the time value of money.

Example #1

Suppose you invest $10,000 today, at a 10% interest rate compounded annually. The annual interest rate is 0.1 (10 divided by 100). After one year, you will have:

$$\text{Amount} = 10000(1 + 0.1)^1$$
$$= \$11{,}000$$

Example #2

Suppose you invest $10,000 today, at a 10% interest rate compounded daily. There are 365 days in a year, so the daily interest rate is about 0.000274 (0.1 divided by 365). After one year, you will have:

$$\text{Amount} = 10000(1 + 0.000274)^{365}$$
$$= 11{,}051.67$$

You should have noticed that the amount invested, the time, and the interest rate for both examples were the same. The only thing that was different was the compounded period. In example #1, the compounding period was annually, which means interest is calculated once per year. In example #2, the compounding period was daily, which means interest is calculated 365 times per year. The more often interest is compounded, the more money you will earn on your investments. These examples illustrate why a sum of money today will accumulate to more money tomorrow.

Compound interest can be your greatest friend but also your worst enemy, because it works the same when you have a loan. If you owe $10,000 today, tomorrow you will owe more, because interest will accrue on that amount. And the more often the interest on the loan is compounded, the faster the debt increases. This is why people who are in debt can quickly sink into deeper debt if they're not paying attention. A daily compounding period, for example, will see your investment start increasing in value from day one, but it will cause your debt to start increasing from day one as well.

It is the lack of understanding of how interest is calculated that causes many people to become slaves to debt. If every student learns these simple concepts in school, the total amount of credit card debt in many countries could be significantly less.

Teach Children About Money and Entrepreneurship

Have you ever wondered why some people work so hard but remain financially poor? Or why some people make good income but cannot afford to purchase a home or even save a few bucks every month? Don't you think this contradicts what you were taught in school? Work hard to get good grades, and you'll get a good job and be successful, and be able to take care of yourself and your family. You may have worked hard in school and got a good job, but do you feel financially successful? If you were to lose your job for six months, would you be able to care for yourself and your family? If your answer is yes, congratulations; you're in the minority. Most people don't have enough saved up to live without a paycheck for even two months. Do you think their situation could have been different if they had been taught the science of money in school—how to make money using multiple strategies, how to invest it and multiply it, and how to have money working for you instead of you having to work for money?

Maslow's hierarchy of needs depicts the needs of humans as a pyramid. At the base of the pyramid are the physiological needs such as food, water, and sleep. Next, there's safety, then love and belongingness, followed by esteem and social needs—confidence, achievement, respect by others—and at the top is self-actualization and realizing your full potential. According to Maslow's theory, the lower order needs should be satisfied, even partially, before the higher order needs can be realized. Now, let's look at the universal needs of people in every society. Would you agree that food, water, shelter, and clothing are at the top of the list of everyone's needs, and that these are the same needs that are at the base of the pyramid? Now, do tell me, which of these needs can be easily satisfied without having money?

So, if money is needed to satisfy these physiological needs, isn't money an essential need for everyone? Don't you think it should be added to the bottom of Maslow's pyramid? Even the young ones, who cannot spend it, need it. They, too, need money to buy their food and clothes, and to provide them with a comfortable home. You may be asking how can the young ones need money if they can't spend it. That's because you do the spending for them. You buy their food and their clothes, and provide the home for them. But as they get older, you pass on some of the responsibilities of satisfying their needs to them, before they even start working. You give them money to buy their lunches, their clothes, and more. So before long, they too will also begin to use money to meet their physiological needs.

Well, if money is such an essential need for everyone, why doesn't everyone learn about the science of money in school? I'm sure you will agree that once you got to a certain age, money became a constant part of your everyday life. You use it every day; you strategize to determine how you can get more of it. You wonder if you'll have enough to feed yourself, to purchase a car, a home, go on a vacation, help your loved ones, and more. But school doesn't prepare you to be financially intelligent. And if you don't have family members who talk openly about money, you really have to learn about it on your own. That sometimes puts you at a disadvantage, because you may make bad choices and realize only after the fact that your decisions about money weren't as wise as you thought prior.

And what about becoming an entrepreneur? Why does the education system, in many countries, not train young people to become entrepreneurs? Why does it focus more on training students to become traditional employees, such as nurses, teachers, lawyers, engineers, and doctors, but not entrepreneurs? Is it because entrepreneurism isn't a worthy profession? That would be absolutely contradicting, because societies benefit considerably from entrepreneurs since they create jobs for employees like you. And if they create jobs, that means our country is benefitting, because more jobs lead to more taxes for our government, and more revenue to provide services for its people.

There should be a balance in the way we teach and train young people in school. Not every student wants to pursue a traditional career to earn money. Some are more interested in making money. Some want to own their own businesses; some want to have a traditional profession and still own a business. Some want to learn about investment strategies and become professional investors. The school system should be looking into the real world to identify the myriad of careers and money-making opportunities available, and have training systems in place to encourage students to pursue studies in all areas of employment and entrepreneurship.

When I was in high school, I loved the sciences, and I did well in them. For this reason, I was timetabled in the science academic stream. I don't remember if we had more than two academic streams then, but I do remember a science and a business one. Being in the science stream, it was very complicated for me to do business and accounting, although those were courses that I wanted to pursue as well. They were in timetable conflict with my science courses. I still remember how disappointed I felt when one of my friends, who was doing principles of business at the time, shared how applicable to life her school base assessment project was, because she could design a business that she dreamed about.

More than 30 years later, and living in a first-world country at that, I still hear students complaining about the same issue: *"I wanted to take this course Ms., but I couldn't because it conflicts with another course that I really want to do as well."* We preach democracy, but are we really giving students the choices to choose what they want? Or are we trying to conform them to an old archaic model that is more than a century behind? Even though I pursued my undergraduate studies in math and computer science, I still wanted to learn about business and accounting. So, a few years after immigrating to Canada, I pursued some business courses at the University of Toronto, which included entrepreneurship, marketing, and accounting. Perhaps it was those courses that were instrumental in spurring me to become an entrepreneur.

Spread the Importance of Financial Education

Many parents start to introduce age-appropriate things, especially relating to literacy and numeracy, to their children before they even begin to speak. They place the highest priority on their children's learning in these two areas. This is their way of giving their children a head start. But would you agree that most parents don't think about giving their children a head start in learning about money and how it works? And why is this? Because, if the schools they attended never taught them financial education, why would they think about preparing their children for something that they never covered in school? Moreover, many parents need financial education themselves, and sometimes those who are financially literate may underestimate how important it is to pass on the lessons, relating to money, to their offspring.

If you are a parent and not financially intelligent, start your financial education today. I shared in the previous chapter about the myriad of resources that are available to help you to become financially literate through self-education. You should commit to begin learning, and as you learn, teach your children about financial education, or get them to learn with you if they're old enough. And if you're already financially educated, talk about matters relating to finances regularly with your children. Every family should talk about money at the dinner table. Children should not only hear their parents talking about money when there is a quarrel relating to who is overspending, or who caused the family to be in debt. If money is a regular topic of discussion at the dinner table, everyone will do their part to practice sound financial conduct and avoid some of the money woes that many families are facing today.

Canada and the United States are two of the wealthiest countries in the world, and more than 35% of the population of both countries have no savings. The combined population of the two countries is more than 368 million at the time of writing this paragraph. So this means, between both countries, more than 128 million people have no savings. That is three and a half times Canada's population alone. So, putting things into perspective, it's like three and a half times the number of people in Canada have no savings, and this is for only two countries. Do you think the situation is better in the rest of the world? And it gets more gloomy, because the report shows that it is as high as 41% in America, and more than 80 million Americans say they don't pay their bills on time. Moreover, the number of Americans who thought it was okay to default on their mortgage was alarming!

Many Canadians and Americans are a paycheck away from not being able to put food on the table for their families. They use credit cards to get through each month, and they carry a balance every month, so they will never be out of debt. Imagine if we had a disaster in multiple industries and some of these people lost employment, who would take care of them and their families? You may be saying that the government would provide unemployment income, or that they could go on social assistance until they find employment. But have you checked the national debt that each country has racked up? Where will the government get the money to sustain these people? And don't forget that thousands of baby boomers are retiring daily and applying for their pensions.

Open your internet browser and type in *Canada's National Debt Clock,* and reflect on the amount you see. Now type in *U.S. National Debt Clock,* and do the same. When I did this exercise on March 18, 2019, Canada's federal debt was more than $685 billion, while America's national debt was close to $22.5 trillion. How did we get to this stage? It's difficult to determine who needs more financial education—consumers or our governments. How can we change this vicious cycle of debt that is plaguing our societies at every level? What can you do to help?

Don't be a part of the statistics, and don't allow your children to be a part of it either. Improve your financial intelligence so that you can stay out of debt or get out of debt as fast as possible. And as you do, financially educate your own children so that they don't make debt their way of life. Many parents work very hard so that their children can enjoy a better life than they had, only to see them leave college in the shackles of debt. Having student loans and relying on old age pension should not be the norm but the exception. Save for your children's tuition, and once they're able to, encourage them to save for their tuition too. Save for rainy days and for your retirement, and encourage your children to begin doing the same as soon as they become employed.

Dare to Leave a Legacy

Everyone should aspire to acquire some wealth so that their families will be okay financially when their time on this Earth expires, especially if it's shorter than expected. Too often, we hear about children having to live in a foster home because a surviving relative is unable to financially care for his or her sibling's children, for example. This often happens when parents fail to build a strong financial foundation for themselves and their families. Usually, it's not intentional, but sometimes they procrastinate, thinking they have enough time to put plans in place, but quite often, it is due to a lack of financial education. School didn't teach them financial literacy, and their parents didn't talk about money, so they know very little about personal finance, and they have a low financial IQ.

There are various strategies that you can use to ensure your family will be taken care of, should disaster strike. But I believe there are six key ones:

1. Life insurance
2. Education savings plan
3. Retirement savings plan
4. Business investments
5. Having a will
6. Financial education

Life Insurance

Napoleon Hill said that at least 10% of your income should go toward your savings, and 10% toward insurance. The first time I listened to *The Law of Success* audiobook, and heard this, I went back 30 seconds because I thought I heard incorrectly. When it was clear that I hadn't, I said out loud: *"Wow, Napoleon…are you saying my savings and my insurance can be considered of equal importance?"* I love Napoleon Hill and his teachings, but I grappled with this statement for a while because, for a long time, I believed my savings were more important than insurance protection, so a higher percentage of my income should go toward savings. Later, when I became more financially intelligent, accumulated more investments, and decided on the type of lifestyle I would like my family to live should misfortune occur, and I took stock of the amount we were spending on life, auto, and home insurance, I realized that Napoleon Hill was definitely correct! I would have been paying more than 10% of my income on insurance if Richard and I didn't have insurance through our employers.

Life insurance will protect your family in the event of unexpected death. All proceeds of the death benefit will go to your family tax-free, providing the beneficiaries are preferred ones like your spouse, children, and parents. And for universal life insurance that has an investment component, your family will receive the investment portion as well; taxes are paid on the interest portion only. The earlier you purchase these insurances, the cheaper they usually are, since you're presumed to be healthier when you're younger. Many people believe money buys insurance when, in fact, it's your health, which is why insurance is much more expensive when you're older. Moreover, the earlier you put these in place, the sooner your family is protected should misfortune occurs.

Education Savings Plan

The sooner you start saving for your children's education, the longer the time the investment has to grow. The government's matching contributions of 20%, as exists in Canada, will have a longer time to grow as well. Hence, there's a greater chance for your investment to increase to your desired amount. Should the benefactor of the savings plan become deceased, the funds will be available to help pay for the education of the beneficiaries. This would help to encourage them to pursue higher education—even in the absence of their parents—since by setting up an education savings plan, the parents would have already planted the seed that their children are expected to attend college. And it could also significantly reduce the amount of student loan they borrow, if more money is needed for tuition.

Retirement Savings Plan

Investing in a retirement savings plan will reduce your income and allow you to defer some tax payments. This tax deferral can prove beneficial to your family in the event of your death. If your beneficiaries are preferred ones, the funds can be transferred to their retirement savings plan. And even though that benefit is not tax-free, like the proceeds of insurance, it will be taxed at the beneficiaries' tax rate whenever they withdraw funds. Their tax rate could be considerably less than yours, which means the money would be taxed at a lower rate than what you would have been taxed at upon retirement.

Business Investments

Starting a business is another great way to leave a legacy for your loved ones. Many successful entrepreneurs have never been an employee. They started a side business from a tender age, like mowing lawns, removing snow, or repairing broken items, and they aspired to become business owners, instead of becoming employees. Hence, upon completing school, they focused their attention on entrepreneurship and strategized to become their own boss. There are many advantages to owning your own business, such as:

1. Lower tax rates
2. Taxes are paid after expenses, unlike an employee
3. Employment for family members
4. Being your own boss

If you involve your family in the business, and teach them how to carry on after your death, the financial impact of your death could be minimal. If the business is a partnership with a non-family member who wishes to carry on in the business with no interference from your family, and you and your partner have a buy-out insurance agreement, upon your death, your partner will give the proceeds from the death benefit to your family, in exchange for your shares in the business. So, your family would fair okay.

Having a Will

Your will is your last testament, and it will ensure that your wishes for your loved ones are carried out even when you're no longer alive. It will tell your executor how your legacy should be allocated. It may also avoid potential conflicts that many families experience upon the death of a loved one. But best of all, it helps to keep the taxman out of your pocket, which means your family gets what you intended for them and not the government.

Financial Education

I have read numerous books about, and listened to, several successful people who failed financially but managed to redeem themselves and achieve more financial success than they did prior to their failure. I have also read numerous books about, and listened to, several successful people who came from impoverished backgrounds. There's one thing that all these people have in common: They have a high level of financial intelligence, and they surround themselves with advisors who have high financial IQ. If you instill the great values of financial education, and the importance of having a strong financial foundation, to your loved ones, and they see that even after death, your will and testament demonstrate that, your loved ones will emulate you and carry on this legacy from generation to generation. A failure to do this may result in them parting quickly with any money that you left for them. But even if a financially educated person and their money are parted, before long, they will find a way to recapture that money, and perhaps significantly more.

Financial Literacy Should Be Mandatory in Schools

Surely, it is understandable why the school system would focus more on training young people to become employees. The more employees a country has, the more income tax the government can collect. But what is the rationale for not teaching our young people financial education? Financial illiteracy doesn't just affect people on an individual level; the collective debt that people incur has an overall effect on the economy of a country, and that of the world as well. I wrote about the national debt clock for Canada and the United States, earlier in this chapter. But why a country would want to advertise its debt to the public, is very mind-boggling for me. Many people feel embarrassed and don't want to talk about the debt that they dig themselves into, because they're not proud of where they are. However, it seems these countries are very pleased with their debt. I was curious to see if other countries were doing the same—did they have a national debt clock too?—and sure enough, other countries were. The United Kingdom's was at £2.1 trillion, France was at €2.2 trillion, and Italy was about €2.1 trillion, to name a few. There seems to be no shame in being in debt, as countries just publicize it to the world.

The writing is on the wall, but these rich countries either turn a blind eye to it, or they refuse to wake up and smell the coffee. They're averted to investing taxpayers' money to develop programs and courses that teach financial education that can be integrated into the school curriculum. They refuse to use taxpayers' money to educate and train teachers to teach financial literacy. Governments prefer to keep most of its citizens financially illiterate and poor so that they can toss them a few fish when they fall on hard times, or when it's election time, and they're soliciting votes. And then say they're there for them in dire situations, instead of financially educating their citizens so that they know how to fish and become much better off in the long run than they are today.

I've said this several times before, but saying it even a million times will still not be sufficient to emphasize that good financial education should be mandatory in school. And the longer governments take to acknowledge this and do something about it, the faster their countries' national debt clocks will tick. And yet sometimes I do wonder if it's a conspiracy among chief stakeholders to keep citizens financially illiterate so that retailers, governments, banks, other financial institutions, and predators in the financial industry can take advantage of citizens. Why do I wonder?

In Canada and the United States, banks collect billions in fees each year from customers because they're not financially intelligent. Credit card companies collect billions in interest and fees from customers yearly because they lack financial education. Governments receive billions in additional sales tax from unnecessary purchases that consumers make each year, because they don't buy smart. Brokers and banks collect billions in fund management fees annually, from financially illiterate investors. Consumers lose billions each year to predators who try to capitalize on their lack of financial education.

Graduates pay millions in student loan interest every year because they and their parents are financially illiterate. The student loan debt in the United States is now sitting at $1.5 trillion, and it is the government's greatest asset. If you calculate the interest on $1.5 trillion, at a rate of 5%, the amount is $75 billion. This means the US government collects more than $75 billion in interest from student loans each year—because some graduates pay as high as 7%—just because these students couldn't afford to pay for their post-secondary education. At the end of 2018, Canadian graduates owed $28 billion in student loan debt, which is also a great asset for the Canadian government as well. If financial education was taught in school, would the student loan debt in Canada and the United States really be that high?

This brings me back to my question: *Is it a conspiracy to exclude financial education from the school curriculum so that the populous is financially illiterate?* I'll let you answer that question.

John McAfee said: *"The ones who are crazy enough to think that they can change the world are the ones who do."* Perhaps I'm crazy enough to think that I can change the world by swinging the financial literacy pendulum. But maybe, with my voice, your voice, the voices of others, and the reach of social media, eventually financial education will be mandatory in every school. And when that happens, the chant will be: "At least 70% of the world's population is financially literate," instead of what I hear now: "At least 70% of the world's population is financially illiterate." So start doing your part to effect change now, and the world will be a better place for our children, grandchildren, and subsequent generations!

Attend Free Financial Education Workshops

World Financial Group – World System Builder

Workshop 1: Increase Cash Flow and Debt Management

Workshop 2: Building a Strong Financial Foundation and Proper Protection

Workshop 3: Building Wealth and Asset Accumulation

Workshop 4: Retirement and Education Planning

Workshop 5: Estate Preservation and Wealth Transfer

Want to Attend a Workshop?

Go to: FinancialLiteracyRocks.com/Workshops

RECOMMENDED READING LIST

Books that support Financial Education and Wealth Building...

Increase Your Financial IQ, by Robert T. Kiyosaki

The Science of Money – How to Create Wealth and Generate Income, by Brian Tracy

A Path to Financial Peace of Mind, by Dwayne Burnell

Rich Dad Poor Dad, by Robert T. Kiyosaki

The Wealthy Barber, by David Chilton

Family Wealth Counseling, by E.G. 'Jay' Link

Second Chance: For Your money, Your life and Our World, by Robert Kiyosaki

Income Investing Secrets, by Richard Stooker

Bank on Yourself, by Pamela Yellen

Why "A" Students Work for "C" Students, by Robert T. Kiyosaki

Becoming Your Own Banker, by R. Nelson Nash

Prescription for Wealth, by Thomas Young

Rich Dad's Cashflow Quadrant, by Robert T. Kiyosaki

Income for Life for Canadians, by Tom Karadza, Nick Karadza, Rob Minton

Life Insurance – Will It Pay When I die? by Thomas Young

Books That support Personal Development and Changing Habits...

Think and Grow Rich, by Napoleon Hill

The 7 Habits of Highly Effective People, by Stephen Covey

The Instant Millionaire, by Mark Fisher

The Richest Man in Babylon, by George S. Clason

The Law of Success, by Napoleon Hill

Start With Why: How Great Leaders Inspire Everyone to Take Action, by Simon Sinek

The Science of Personal Achievement, by Napoleon Hill

Focal Point: A Proven System to Simplify Your Life, by Brian Tracy

Ready, Fire, Aim: Zero to $100 Million in No Time Flat, by Michael Masterson

How to Stop Worrying and Start Living, by Dale Carnegie

The Organized Mind: Thinking Straight in the Age of Information Overload, by Daniel J. Levitin

Fake: Fake Money, Fake Teachers, Fake Assets, by Robert Kiyosaki

RECOMMENDED WEBSITES FOR FINANCIAL EDUCATION

Free financial literacy workshops through World Financial Group – https://www.youtube.com/watch?v=TFD0EPwbdUQ

Smart About Money – http://www.onyourown.org/

Financial Consumer Agency of Canada – http://www.fcac-acfc.gc.ca/Eng/financialLiteracy/Pages/home-accueil.aspx

Personal finance and the rush to competence – http://www.isfs.org/documents-pdfs/rep-finliteracy.pdf

Federal Deposit Insurance Corporation. Money Smart– A financial education program – https://www.fdic.gov/consumers/consumer/moneysmart/adult.html

A survey of financial literacy among university students –http://journal.mufad.org.tr/attachments/article/767/11.pdfSmart

A Joint Publication by Russia's G20 Presidency and the OECD. Advancing National Strategies for Financial Education – http://www.oecd.org/finance/financial-education/G20_OECD_NSFinEd_Summary.pdf

ABOUT INGRID B. CLAYTON

Ingrid B. Clayton is an award-winning author, a wife, and a mother of two sons. She's also an educator, a property manager, and a real estate investor, owning properties in Canada and the United States. She has a Bachelor of Science degree in math and computer science from the University of the West Indies, Jamaica, and a Master's in Education from Yorkville University, Canada. She taught at the Queen's School, in Jamaica, from 1997 to 2000; then she migrated from Jamaica to Canada, in 2000, where she continued her teaching career with the Toronto District School Board. She has more than twenty-three years of experience teaching high school math and computer science, and she's currently the assistant curriculum leader of mathematics at Lester B. Pearson Collegiate in Scarborough, Canada.

Over the last few years, Ingrid has seen the increasingly devastating effects that debt and other unwise financial decisions bring to families. She believes this is a result of a lack of financial education because consumers weren't taught financial literacy skills in school. Many families don't even talk about money anymore, because it often conjures up unpleasantries that most people prefer to keep buried. Ingrid believes that if financial literacy is no longer taught in the homes, then it should be incorporated into the educational system in every country. And the longer governments take to acknowledge this, and do something about it, the more the debt crisis epidemic will continue to affect families' finances and the world's economy.

She has made it her life's goal to change the education system to include teachings on personal finance and the basics of living financially wise, which covers saving and investing, budgeting, good and bad debt, doing taxes, and practicing smart buying and spending habits. She became a member of World Financial Group – World System Builder, in 2019, to join their Financial Literacy Campaign to financially educate one million families by the end of 2020. Ingrid believes that consumers should be educated and given choices before they make decisions on financial undertakings, and that was Xuan Nguyen's objective when he founded World System Builder. Ingrid now works as a training associate with a team of trainers at World System Builder, to financially educate families and help them to build a strong financial foundation.

Ingrid is also creating financial literacy courses to help young adults get the training they need so that they can avoid bad decisions, or reverse the beginning of the debt cycle before it becomes irreversible. She and her husband have worked hard to create the life they want to live by increasing their financial IQ, and making good investments in real estate and other asset classes. Now she wants to help others, especially young people, to become financially intelligent so they can escape the trap of the debt cycle, get out of the rat race quickly, and live financially free.

ABOUT THIS BOOK

I wrote this book because I believe the debt situation that many families are experiencing, and the debt crisis that many countries are facing, could have been avoided. And yet I think it is still not too late to remedy this problem and change the trajectory of the younger generation—and subsequent ones—if the appropriate measures are taken by governments and everyone else to effect this change, because there is a solution…Financial Education.

I believe we live in a rich country with enough resources and wealth so that no one should be living poor. Many people are living in poverty because of financial illiteracy, and governments should be grossly blamed for this. The education system in every country should play a vital role in equipping young people with the necessary knowledge and skills to make informed decisions about matters to do with their finances. When education policymakers refused to make financial education mandatory in school, essentially, they sentenced young people to a lifestyle that is laden with debt and disappointments, and for this reason, many families are hurting today.

The purpose of this book is threefold: First, to explain why academic success doesn't tantamount to financial success, why there are many high academic achievers who struggle with managing their finances effectively and are drowning in debt, and what governments should do to financially educate the populous so that they can build a strong financial foundation. Secondly, to share some basics about financial literacy, to illustrate how financial education can impact your decisions and your mindset about money, and the positive impact that a higher level of financial intelligence will have on your lifestyle and the lifestyle of your loved ones. And lastly, to share some stories from my personal experiences as to how I came to realize that I needed to increase my financial IQ, what I did upon the realization, the difference that a higher level of financial intelligence made for me and my loved ones, and what we can all do to improve our financial education to help our family members and change the financial journey for the next generation.

Many of us have heard the saying: *"The love of money is the root of all evil."* There's also the other one that says: *"Money cannot make you happy; happiness comes from within."* But I would like to propose these questions: Do people actually love money, or do they love the freedom that money can afford them? Don't you feel happy when you can provide for your family the way you want to, contribute to a charity that is dear to your heart, and help relatives and friends who may need some financial assistance? Can you accomplish these feats without money? Does struggling to provide for your family, or living from paycheck to paycheck makes you happy? As you journey through this book, my intention is that you will commit to building a strong financial foundation to become financially free, and start living life on your own terms as quickly as possible.

www.ingramcontent.com/pod-product-compliance
Lightning Source LLC
Chambersburg PA
CBHW050555170426
43201CB00011B/1708